THE
WILD WOMAN'S
BOOK OF
SHADOWS

A Magical Guide of Rituals + Practices
for Living an Enchanted Life

MELISSA KIM CORTER

AND 22 WILD WOMEN FROM ACROSS THE GLOBE

THE WILD WOMAN'S BOOK OF SHADOWS

A Magical Guide of Rituals + Practices for Living an Enchanted Life

By Melissa Kim Corter

Ordering Information: Quantity sales. Special discounts are available on quantity purchases. For details, contact the publisher. Programs, products, or services provided by the authors are found by contacting them directly.

Published by Wild Woman Ink
https://dev.melissacorter.com/product/wild-womans-book-of-shadows

Book Design by Shanda Trofe

ISBN: 978-0-578-91625-5

Printed in the United States of America

To every woman here and gone. To the ones who were
silenced, suppressed, or afraid to speak up and honor the
sacred echoes in their hearts ... we hear you and
feel you in our bones.
Thank you ... your presence and lives opened
invisible doors of possibility.

CONTENTS

BECOMING THE WILD WOMAN

Melissa Kim Corter
(aka Luna Grace)

Luna Grace was born the moment she retrieved her power from the shadows haunting her mind. It became her mission to shake shit up, like a modern-day Kali with a more gentle and less threatening approach. Instead of cracking the foundation beneath her feet, Luna Grace claimed her path by dancing between worlds and wielding light among the doubt and insecurity. In this chapter, I help you find your own Wild Woman, the way the essence of Luna Grace channeled through me to remind other women of the magic flowing through their veins.

Your Wild Woman may have been disgraced, abandoned, or rejected; she may have been hidden, suppressed, or broken. Still, she knows her magic and refuses to settle for anything less than extraordinary. She has the audacity to be unapologetically herself. She pulls the parts of her soul back from the trenches, places they were left or forgotten. She doesn't try to become fearless; instead, she's the alchemist of fear, transforming it into the wands of her words, creating magic, weaving dreams, and channeling grace into everything she touches.

Before the essence of Luna Grace can appear among these pages, she must first share the darkness – spaces she hid in and shadows she once called home. Melissa lived in fear for many years. She felt everything so deeply, and she saw spirits and energy. Others didn't understand her empathic and intuitive gifts; they were too serious and drowning in sorrows, completely disconnected from the body. Melissa was taught by those around her to hide her light, to stop talking, stop feeling so much and she morphed into what was expected of her. She stopped telling her vibrant stories, she stopped talking about the shadows and their secrets; she only shared with the one feminine influence she felt safe with: the moon. Melissa was alone, and the only time she felt peace was when she went into the woods There, among the trees and rocks, Melissa could connect, cry, and wander. The woods were alive with wisdom and answers, sometimes drifting into her mind from the wind, other times coming up from the Earth.

Retrieving power from a person, situation, or memory allows life to take on a new sense of vibrancy. I'll share a client experience as a beautiful example. This client (I'll call her Rose to protect her privacy) came as a referral after her friend shared the details of her session with me. The friend explained how I utilized my intuition to read her nervous system to find patterns and connections to past events. Rose was struggling and wanted this for herself. As we spoke I dialed into her energy and immediately sensed her soft and gentle nature; I was also receiving tons of information streaming through me. So I asked her, "Who are you waiting to receive permission from?" There was silence on the other end of the phone and I knew my question had caught her off guard. She was pulling back, questioning the process. Gently, I kept going, sharing more information as I retrieved it from her, until I pinpointed a specific moment when Rose was six years old.

She was at her friend Amy's house, a few houses down from her own. The two were playing quietly in Amy's room when the front door slammed. It was Amy's father and he was angry. A second later they heard him and Amy's mother yelling at each other. Rose felt instantly sick and wanted to go home but she was afraid to leave. The arguing continued while Rose cried and told Amy she wanted to go home. Amy said, "No, you're staying here with me. I don't like when they fight and you can't leave me by myself." Rose reluctantly stayed, and remained in complete fear the entire time. Eventually the arguing stopped and Rose told Amy she needed to get home for supper. Amy believed her and let her go.

Fast forward to the present moment. Rose has struggled her entire life to have boundaries, express her needs, and make decisions for herself. Every time she found herself in a situation requiring her to stand in her power and use her voice, she felt crippling anxiety and needed to escape immediately. Rose found herself lying to get out of things and felt ashamed by this behavior; however, she had never connected her resistance or ongoing patterns with that long-ago moment at Amy's.

We traced the emotions in her system to the six-year-old self, and they were identical. In the original event Rose felt panic and anxiety; her body froze and she shut down the overwhelming fear when she was told she couldn't leave. It was crucial for Rose to recognize that she believed she needed permission to do so. All of these feelings were the same in the present moment, over thirty-five-years later. Hearing me reflect the energy to her resonated so deeply that she broke down in tears. She'd had no idea that this event was repeating in her daily life until this profoundly insightful moment. Together, we found her magic, healed the fear, and reclaimed Rose's power and voice.

To become the Wild Woman, we must first see her as our authentic self – not as an outcast, not as a problem child or bad girl; and not as someone who will draw negative attention and criticism. The Archetype of the Wild Woman was first brought to my awareness by Dr. Clarissa Pinkola Estes, in her book *Women who Run with Wolves.* I think of the Wild Woman as intuitive, wonderful, wise, connected, divine, magical, and mystical. She is filled with the divine and knows her power to create the reality she lives in. She has a shadow just as all of the archetypes do, yet she doesn't fear her shadow; she walks directly into it, for she knows it holds information for her to learn from.

Archetypes are constructs, or roles we innately have the potential to express and live out. For example, if you were to describe the Martyr, you might think of someone who does things for attention to receive praise for giving all of themselves to a cause or dynamic. If you were to describe the Outlaw, you might think of someone who never follows rules, cannot be tamed, and ignores the boundaries of acceptable behaviors. Many women struggle to find themselves, and to become an authentic version of who they are called to be.

Women also grapple with – and this is a big one! – not knowing how to receive.

The Wild Woman knows how to give AND receive without compromising herself

We all have the potential within us to embody any archetype; life has a way of invoking various roles during a particular phase of life or during times of need. Exploring the Wild Woman for yourself is a personal journey. She is within you; she holds magic, power, grace and divinity.

There are three main elements I work with to help clients get in touch with their inner Wild Woman:

Uncovering: Observing, sifting, clearing, and releasing various layers of suppression and avoidance. She's there within you, a small voice waiting to be heard and hoping you will one day stop tuning away from her.

Unlearning: Deciding, opening, expanding, and integrating new truths, not just those inherited or absorbed from the world around us. She invites you to release all you've been taught to embody all you see and desire to weave in your world.

Untethering: Healing, transforming, shedding, and assimilating your deepest desires and joy-filled expressions into physical form while still here in a body. Creating from Heaven and Earth while discarding the tethers and ties of limiting beliefs and ways of being.

To begin this process of uncovering, unlearning, and untethering, you will need a few things:

1. A journal and pen.

2. A safe, quiet, still place for you to be completely present and without disruption.

3. An open heart and mind.

4. The discipline to follow through on this exercise, meaning you don't just read the words but let them come alive within your experience.

Becoming the Wild Woman

Take a few minutes to connect to your breath. I teach my clients how to do box breathing which allows the body to shift into a parasympathetic state (rest, digest, ease, comfort, relaxation) while also slowing brainwaves to achieve an altered state of consciousness.

For box breathing, follow this series of prompts:

1. Inhale to the count of four

2. Hold for four seconds

3. Exhale to the count of four

4. Pause for four seconds

5. Repeat this cycle for a minimum of four rounds of breathing

Now close your eyes and imagine you are deep in the forest. You hear the echo of a wolf howling and instinctively know it is a "she" and that she's calling you to her. Feeling a little panicky, you run through the woods trying to find her, but the faster you run the further the howling falls away. The howling vibrates throughout your body, and you begin to crave it. You want it close, and you want to be in her presence, yet she eludes you.

You finally pause – tired, out of breath, ego worn down – and sit on the Earth. As you catch your breath, trying to figure out the next plan of action, a sense of defeat washes over you. The howling has softened and the she-wolf seems to have vanished. A part of you weeps for her in despair, and then your spirit invites you to surrender. You surrender your need to find her and detach from the outcome. You let go.

A sense of comfort returns, and you stand up and plant your feet firmly on the ground. Something begins to stir within – a tiny whisper at first – and before you can contain it, the most visceral calling of your soul emerges. It is a primordial scream, feminine in its energetic signature; you rise and feel your body shake, your muscles ache, and the howl escapes your lips.

After what feels like an eternity, you soften. It brings you to tears to recognize you have been chasing your own shadow. She was never "out there"; she was always in HERE, waiting for you to let her speak. The worn-down ego and the fatigue of the hustle brought you to the space to finally see her, hear her, sense her...*be her.*

Now, you are ready to begin writing. This writing invites deep and hidden pockets of creativity to surface so you can receive it. Continue to monitor your breathing in a relaxed manner. Let it be easy and guided instead of controlled.

Begin writing to your inner Wild Woman, thank her, apologize to her, learn from her. Ask her questions:

- Who am I, really? Deep beneath societal or family behaviors and belief systems?
- What do I crave that I am not allowing myself to have?
- How do I embody the Wild Woman?
- What beliefs do I hold preventing me from accessing her?
- How can I honor her going forward?

Unlearning is a process; for some it is a swift quick shift, for others it is grueling or intimidating. Regardless, she needs you and is waiting for you to stop abandoning her. Who is she? What is the name of your Wild Woman? Mine is Luna Grace: fierce and gentle, insightful and powerful, intense yet humble. The final piece is to sit in stillness, and ask her to reveal her name to you. It doesn't need to make sense, or seem like a normal human name. This process may involve layers, so be gentle and willing to listen without chasing her; just let her pour through you. Chasing, grasping, forcing, and trying to make her appear will ensure she fades away. Love the tender places you fear, sit with them, invite them to teach you and they always will. She who knows her magic can never be tamed; she can only be awakened.

Melissa Kim Corter is a best-selling author, intuitive coach, and clinical hypnotherapist certified in over thirty-six modalities. She holds a bachelor's degree in psychology and is currently pursuing her doctorate. Her specialty is overcoming emotions that sabotage prosperity, visibility, and success with her evidence-based approach. Melissa has a unique ability to uncover blockages and self-defeating patterns cycling through the nervous system and subconscious mind. Once she hones in on the specific issues at hand and has found the pattern, she crafts a recipe for her clients to release and replace the block with hypnosis and EFT (Emotional Freedom Technique).

Melissa has helped many creatives, authors, and coaches to release their fears and achieve their goals. For more than seventeen years, Melissa has extensively studied many facets of intuition, neuroscience, human behavior, shamanism, and spirituality. She is the author of Nudges from Your Spirit and the creator of the Intuitive Tapping Method™.

www.melissacorter.com

THE NURTURING NIGHT OF THE SOUL

Becky Woods

"Welcome, dear one. I have been expecting you. Oh, how I cherish our time together. It's always a lovely time of remembering, rediscovering and expressing yourself in all your glory. These moments fan the flame, fuel the fire and warm the bones. One day we will walk this life hand in hand and create magic beyond your dreams."

~ Soul

In a society that has conditioned us to think more and do more, we have forgotten how to feel and be. We have forgotten that we need to nurture and honor our souls. Though this is still a sacred practice for women in many cultures around the world, it has largely been forgotten in the U.S., with significant effects on our wellbeing.

As a divorced working mom, I too struggled with putting down the thinking-more and doing-more mentality, yet I was too busy and too tired to figure out another way. I spent most of my twenties and thirties in survival mode, raising four children and often ignoring my own needs and feelings. Feelings were a luxury I didn't have time for; after all, being a mom meant my life was on hold until they all turned eighteen, right? Wrong! Somewhere in my mid-thirties I realized something had to change and I was the only one who could change it.

I tried many things and learned something from each of them. The Nurturing Night of the Soul, which I will share with you here, is a combination of techniques that have helped me heal. It has truly been a life-changer, and my wish is that we can pass it down to our children and grandchildren earlier in their lives so they create more magic and positive change in our world.

This ritual will empower you to support and nurture yourself while also learning to slow down and get in touch with your soul. You will learn to give yourself permission to change and allow things to be different. The more time you spend in this nurturing space, the more you will remember what truly brings passion and meaning into your life. You will start to reconnect with nature. You will start to purposefully practice gratitude, and how to be present and honor yourself. This, my friends, is magic!

One of the things I love about The Nurturing Night of the Soul is the abundance of versatility and opportunities to make it your own. Each time it can be new and different. You are welcome to elaborate on and adjust it as you feel called. I have given you a foundation to build upon – the key building blocks to unlock the magic. Listen to your soul for guidance and practice. The more you practice and get comfortable, the more magic you will create. Plan at least an hour of uninterrupted time and space. An entire evening is ideal, but any amount of time is beneficial, which is why I also offer a shortened version that you can use on a more regular basis.

The preparation for this ritual is minimal. The idea is to keep your mind on its purpose – nurturing your soul – even while performing the preparations. Here is what you'll need:

- Water to drink. Your body is made up of 60% water. Water is a conductor of energy. Therefore, it is easier to sense subtle energy shifts if you are properly hydrated.
- A package of unscented tealight candles and candleholders. Never leave open flames unattended (you may substitute battery candles or other dim glowing lighting).
- 1-3 cups of bath salts. If you have metal plumbing or are unsure what kind of plumbing you have, I suggest Epsom salt. Epsom Salt is magnesium sulfate ($MgSo4$) and won't cause rusting of metal pipes like sodium chloride ($NaCl$) salt will.
- Essential oil or a scented candle. For cleansing energy I suggest eucalyptus; for relaxation I recommend ashwagandha or lavender.
- Soothing background music without lyrics. Try spa, Reiki or meditation music to get started.
- A lighter or matches

As you prepare for this ritual, trust and believe that the energy you invest in yourself will come back to you manyfold. Once we remember that we are the only ones responsible for nurturing our soul and that it is an honor and privilege to do so, we are free! We no longer rely on external people, factors, opinions or circumstances to determine how we feel and how we proceed in life. We realize our role as co-creators of our ideal reality. Yes! It is that profound and it can be that easy.

There are certain times throughout the year in which the Universe has an abundant supply of supportive energy to offer to you. The times that would most benefit you while performing this ritual include full and new moon phases as well as the solstices and equinoxes. Although these are potent times, I would never suggest limiting your rituals to them. The more you are in communion with your soul the more you will heal, grow and expand.

You may enjoy picking up some fresh flowers to enjoy during your ritual, and to serve as a great remembrance of your special time in the days that follow. I also like to have a favorite beverage and snack available. Spoil yourself a little bit.

Begin by turning off any unnecessary background noise and turning on your music in the bathroom. Also in the bathroom, start placing the candles in a way that allows you to safely bathe by candlelight. You will also want to place them in all the rooms you plan to be in. You may want a few larger pillar candles in some areas. Also, plan to carry one from room to room. After you have placed the candles, light your carry candle. Give thanks for the element of fire. On your way back to the bathroom, start to shut off the lights. As you shut off the lights, give thanks for technology and the ease of modern living.

Once you have returned to the bathroom, close the door and light all your candles in this room. Then shut off the lights. Now you are ready to place the drain stopper in the tub and start running the water. I recommend <u>not</u> turning on the bathroom fan. Just allow the steam to build up like a sauna. It's good for your skin and lungs, as well as the ambiance. As the water is running sprinkle in your salts. Give thanks for the earth and its minerals. Then add the essential oils or light your scented candle.

If you prefer showering over a bath, follow the same steps and shower with the drain stopper in, if possible. (If you don't have a tub/shower combo, use a diffuser for the essential oils and a body wash with the salts included.)

While you undress, imagine all of your duties and stress peeling away with your clothes. As you enter the water, feel how it surrounds you. Water carries memories and will carry away any energies that no longer serve you. Feel how the water supports and holds you. Give thanks for the element of water. While in this space, tune into your senses. What do you smell, hear, feel? Does your bathroom look different in the candlelight? Watch the flames and shadows for a while. Listen to the music. Just feel and be. Thank yourself for investing this time into your wellbeing.

When you are ready to exit the water, say to yourself or aloud, "Thank you, Water, for taking all the energies that no longer serve me to Mother Earth, to be transmuted and transformed into love and light, for the highest good of all." Start to drain the water and visualize any stress or worries going down the drain. As you dry off, think of a reason you are thankful for each area of your body. Remember to grab your carry candle and extinguish the other candles before leaving each room unattended. This is usually where I end the ritual for the shortened version. I also limit the candles to the bathroom.

Now is also a great time to apply oils or lotions and don your lounge wear for the evening. (or lack of … up to you!)

This is when I usually grab a beverage and gaze out my window at the stars, open the window and listen to the wind or just sit in my comfy chair and watch the flames flicker and the shadows dance for a bit. Does it feel as though you have managed to stop time? How different do your surroundings look in the candlelight and stillness? This is the magic! You have transformed your day-to-day space into a sacred temple for your soul. Enjoy this space as long as you can. Soak it up. Breathe it in.

Then ask your soul what it needs more of. The first thing that you hear is the answer. Make a promise to yourself to bring more of "that" into your daily life. You may also choose to do an activity by candlelight, such as read, journal or paint. The sky's the limit!

When you decide it is time to retire, start blowing out all your candles. Stop at each one and watch the smoke for just a few seconds and be thankful for this time of remembering and nurturing.

You are able to create this magic as often as you wish. As you lay down, close your eyes and drift off to sleep, let your heart be filled with gratitude and overflow with love. May you have the sweetest of dreams and know that you are cherished and held in love and light. And so it is.

Becky Woods is an Intuitive Life Coach, a Level 3 Reiki practitioner, and psychic medium. As an intuitive youngster she was always interested in the unknown, a passion she still has today. She loves learning everything she can about energy and believes that magic is science that just isn't understood … yet. The great part is that you don't have to understand it for it to work!

Becky has made a lifelong study of various cultures, religions and their practices. She uses her science background, insight, intuition, multiple modalities and education in energy work to tap into those places in the body that are in a state of dis-ease. She then intuitively chooses a process to shift them back to a state of ease. She is also able to clear spaces and auras, balance chakras and restore flow to slowed or blocked energy pathways.

After working with Becky, her clients often mention feeling an overall sense of peace and relaxation. Many feel a major positive shift in mood, mindset and energy levels, and often have an emotional release that leaves them feeling much lighter.

Becky grew up in a small farming community in Minnesota, which she still calls home. For over sixteen years she has been a Medical Laboratory Technician, though she has worked in many other fields as well. She even took a break from the lab to acquire her Commercial Driver's License and drive a gravel truck for six years! She enjoys spending time with her family and friends but feels most at peace when she is out in nature. She also loves travelling, singing, dancing, writing, painting, ice-fishing, and riding her Harley!

www.energeezinc.com

EnerGeezInc@gmail.com

HEALING WATERS:
A DAILY RITUAL

Brandi Strieter

Moving energy through my body is an integral part of my health and wellness routine. It begins upon waking in the morning, when I visualize pulling the energy down into my physical body, through the chakras, and continues throughout the day with intentional physical movement and earthing. However, my evening routine has helped me to learn the foundational practice of unconditional self-love which was the catalyst for change in the direction of my life. The simplicity and predictability of a nighttime bath with water meditation was the vehicle in which I learned to surrender my ego mind and tap into my higher self. Although I no longer require water or meditation to receive spiritual guidance, it was this daily practice of connection, using the element of water as an incubator, that propelled me forward in my consciousness development.

Before I go into the bath experience, I feel it's important to share that I wasn't always aware of my connection to Spirit and for decades I lived a life that was completely void of self-love. In truth, I spent years rooted in separation and disassociation from my higher self. Looking back, I understand I was simply living on autopilot after years of suppressing unprocessed emotions. This arose from experiencing a childhood where codependency was modeled, and self-love was absent.

Unaware of my disconnect, I entered into a career in law enforcement, absorbing the traumatic energy around me while battling infertility, pregnancy loss, and advocating for a special needs child at home. Not surprisingly, I had also become dependent on antidepressants to numb the pain without ever addressing the root issue, and physical manifestations began to surface in my body.

A non-healing foot fracture that caused immobility for sixteen months was the first indicator that my body had been keeping score. It was also during this time that my mother prematurely transitioned to Spirit. These two difficult life experiences gave me the courage to start asking questions about my purpose, and begin to dip my toes in spirituality.

A stem cell surgery was performed on my ailing foot, and though it was deemed a success, a couple of weeks later I became extremely ill. First, my hearing was affected, then my eyesight, and finally my body began to shut down, giving me unimaginable physical pain. A few weeks later, I was only a shell of the person that I once was. Western medicine proved to be my greatest teacher, not that I thought of it this way at the time. Its only offerings were more surgeries or medications for symptom relief and I was ultimately labeled as attention-seeking and delusional. The journey to a medical diagnosis took over a year and a half and resulted in severe emotional trauma. I was left feeling completely alone and unsupported, which was exactly what I needed to experience for me to hit rock bottom and surrender my ego.

It was in the middle of this fight for my life that I remember-ed my earlier introduction to spirituality and the angelic realm, so I asked for some assistance. It was then that I began to trust there was purpose in my pain and even to believe that I would survive in order to help others.

With intuitive guidance, I was led to an amazing naturopathic doctor who introduced me to the world of holistic medicine. For a girl raised on antibiotics, vaccines, and Dr. Spock the alternative healing world was eye-opening, and for over eighteen months I dove headfirst into learning how to heal my physical body. As I reclaimed my power and sovereignty, I knew that the trajectory of my life had changed, and I was unwilling to return to stuffing my emotions. My life began to depend on a new set of guidelines, and I discovered the true value of self-love.

I share the depth of my personal despair in order for you to understand the significance that the sacred bath played in my eventual awakening. It is where I finally conceded the battle with my soul and invited my higher self into an embodied experience which led to my healing and recovery.

You may be wondering what self-love and a bath have in common, so I'll explain. Never in my life had I valued myself enough to make time for my own needs. I longed to feel un-conditional love for myself and eventually understood that the first step was to create time and space dedicated solely for me. In my healing journey, I was fortunate to have the opportunity to learn from many different healers and diverse modalities and found value in using water in detoxification. It's essential when clearing the body of toxins to not only unblock the dense energy but to also assist in releasing the energy from the body and its tissues. There are countless different ways to help and support the body, but I enjoyed the consistency of a regular detox bath that I could perform in my home.

I initially told myself the nightly bath routine was a "medical necessity" – this is how uncomfortable it was for me to make myself a regular priority! To make it more appealing, I also incorporated my knowledge of the various therapeutic benefits of gemstones and infused the bath water with high vibrational energy and then, I moved my newly established meditation practice to water as well.

Always surrounding me, I know, was Spirit, the Angels, and my guides but they all felt too distant; however, my connection to my higher self was developing nicely. Through that blossoming relationship, which was for once based on unconditional love and self-forgiveness, I was guided to surrender control of my ego and become open to receiving the powerful exchange of healing energy through the safety and security of a home bath meditation.

There are various interpretations of a sacred bath and how to best utilize the womb of water to connect and recharge. I like to begin with a basic core bath, which is just a general guideline, and then I customize from there each day, taking into consideration what I have available, and also adding things to assist my ever-changing emotional and physical needs.

I begin every session by ensuring that I am being intentional and present in the bath preparation, because that is just as important as the healing experience itself. I would also encourage you to reflect on what you want your bath goals to be each time. Often, I wish to focus on healing my body, or sending healing to others. Sometimes I seek galactic connection and guidance and other times I choose to just relax and recharge. Tune into your own body and feel the wisdom it has to offer to you.

After setting your intentions, fill the tub with water while being mindful of the temperature. Warmer water can always be added once you are in the tub. I like to add a variety of gemstones to the water at this point and my personal favorites are sodalite and selenite. A sodalite stone in the bath assists with clearing the body of negative energies as well as purifying the aura. I also love adding selenite powder, which promotes harmony and brings into oneself a feeling of peace.

Now that the crystals are marinating, I light three candles. I prefer my baths in the moonlight or candlelight as the darkness allows me to focus more easily on my connection rather than getting distracted by looking at my body. I also like to burn moldavite, an incense which helps to awaken the senses and invites in the energy of inner-dimensional knowledge.

Once the tub is full and the water infused with crystal energy, I add a generous amount of Epsom salt, which helps to remove toxins and aids in healing. I will also add several drops of eucalyptus or other essential oils. For a full moon bath, I also include four tablespoons of grated ginger and bentonite clay as directed on the package. Both assist in detoxification of the body.

Selecting the music is the final act of preparation. For some baths I am called to chant or listen to a guided meditation; for others I prefer the simplicity of the gentle sound of running water or spa music.

After a quick shower to cleanse and prepare my body, I slip into the water, close my eyes, and immediately feel like I'm wrapped in a cocoon of love. As a Reiki Master, I use symbols to invoke healing and begin to drop into the quantum energy field. Breath is vital in order to open up the meridians and move the energy through the body, so I spend some time in intentional deep breathing. Being open, I lay my hands on my face, covering my eyes to aid in grounding and using my third eye, I visualize my crown chakra opening at the top of my head and imagine a plug extending to my higher self, securing them together.

At this point, you can invite in your team of light into the now moment for your highest good, asking them to share what you need to know and remember. Then, settle into your body and trust your team is coming in, surrounding you and honoring you.

Imagine a circle of light being formed around your body and use your breath to move the energy through your body as well.

To remain present and anchored, focus on each of your five senses. Feel the high vibrational energy as it moves through your body like an electrical current and lean into the frequency of love. Allow the light inside you to form around your body and receive the healing energies. Encourage that exchange of information between dimensions and also communicate your needs. If you notice your mind wandering, return it to your five senses and take notice of what you can see, hear, and feel. Slowly, and over time, lengthen how long you spend in this sacred space.

After some practice and consistency, you will be able to anchor into this peaceful feeling easily. It can be an effective form of meditation and will help you to master the releasing of all thoughts that surface with grace and ease, allowing other information to become available to you. While in this relaxed state, using my mind's eye, I visualize myself laying on a raft, in a lagoon filled with crystal blue water, next to a lush, green mountain. I can hear the sounds of birds chirping in the distance and feel a cool breeze on my skin.

It was in this space where I felt safe and supported for the first time, and for weeks I was thrilled with that new visual and the feeling that enveloped me while I was there. I thought of it as my own little nirvana. Then, one day, I was joined by my guides, who invited me to go on a galactic journey. After that, it didn't take long for my third eye lagoon to become a portal into other worlds. It always begins, however, with the bath and meditation. Since my first trip to the quantum field, I have been gifted with other-worldly knowledge and wisdom often beyond my understanding. My connection with Spirit has strengthened as well and my intuition has skyrocketed, thus the channeling and mediumship that followed is forever expanding.

Reflecting back on my circular journey to self, I am grateful for the simplicity in the ritual bath and the grounding foundation it provided me. I understand now that before I could journey into the ethereal skies, I first had to become rooted in my body, in this present moment on earth. I'm eternally thankful for the guidance of the healers before me who loved me unconditionally until I was able to see my own light, and I'm honored to now hold space for others as they venture into the unknown waters to their own freedom. I encourage all of you to allow yourself to experience the time, space, and consistency of a nurturing daily bath and meditation and hope that it may be the beginning of a beautiful new relationship with your higher self and the Spirit realm. The water is waiting for you.

Brandi Strieter is an Intuitive Guide, Energy Healer and certified Mind, Body, Spirit Practitioner. For several years she walked an eventful journey through hopelessness and despair while struggling with the painful and debilitating symptoms of undiagnosed chronic Lyme Disease. That journey led her into surrendering and finally, ultimate freedom. Brandi has since vowed to never let another soul suffer the same fate and she has made it her purpose to shine light for those in the darkness. She now assists others seeking true alignment by utilizing her knowledge and wisdom of many diverse spiritual teachers, as well as her own ideologies and intuitive guidance around energy healing and the mind, body, spirit connection.

Since 2016, Brandi has mentored under transformational thought leader Sunny Dawn Johnston and is proud to be the Community Ambassador to ELEV8, Sunny's international membership community, as well as her Social Media Specialist. Brandi resides in Arizona with her husband, two sons, and three German Shepherds.

www.brandistrieter.com

www.facebook.com/BrandiStrieterBiz

IS IT IN THE FAMILY?

Cindy Merriam

Mom and Dad knew each other's families when they were young; then again, everybody knew everybody in the small farming community where they grew up. Mom still loves to tell the story of the freezing winter day when she was hit by a snowball. Guess who threw it? That was the beginning of their love story, and it came as no surprise to anyone when a few years later they got married.

The newlyweds honeymooned in northern Michigan, which is where my dad's Great-Aunt Grace lived. Aunt Grace was one of a kind. She had survived the Depression; outlived three husbands – the last of whom drowned in a boating accident on Lake Michigan – and buried a twenty-year-old grandson. The last loss took a lot out of her, but she was always welcoming and never lost her smile. But there was something else that was special about Aunt Grace: she was a very gifted psychic.

While my parents were there she did a reading for Mom. No reading is perfect, but she intuited a long, happy marriage and three children, followed by a surprise baby. Indeed, within the space of three years, Mom gave birth to three kids – me, my sister Karen, and my brother Trevor. Imagine our surprise when a baby, Matthew, was born ten years after Trevor!

Aunt Grace often faced the religious objections of others but continued her readings in spite of it. In fact, people traveled from all over Michigan and Wisconsin to get a reading from her. She used a regular deck of cards, and I can tell you she intuited some things you would not believe. There was even a newspaper article written about her. Matthew referred to her as "Poor Old," but looking back she was probably only in her sixties at the time. She was the original Wild Woman.

My family visited her several times when I was growing up. She really wanted to read "my fortune," as she called it, but I didn't let her because I was skeptical and a little scared. Yet each time she did a reading for one of my family members, she would start to include me in it until Mom reminded her that she had discarded the card that represented me. One time she was reading Trevor and told him be quiet. Trevor said, "Okay" and Aunt Grace said, "Trevor, I said be quiet," and again Trevor said, "Okay." This happened four or five times before my brother caught on and we all had a good laugh. She really was very funny.

Aunt Grace was a lifelong smoker and walked with an oxygen tank. It never occurred to us that this practice was dangerous, that is, until I got married and my husband mentioned it. Buzz kill! She died of natural causes at the age of ninety, and without having read me.

In 1980 I moved to Minneapolis and became friends with Stephanie, a woman I worked with. I was still single at the time and so was she, so we spent a lot of time together. I remember starting to notice different things at work. One day, after seeing a few people in the Human Resources office, I returned to the department Stephanie and I worked in and told her she was going to be given a new opportunity. Later that day she was promoted to a new position. I recognized the managers in the HR office and thought I had just put two and two together. It never occurred to me that I had intuited it.

Time passed and we both changed jobs. One night we were out for dinner with a few friends and the conversation turned to morning journaling and meditation. Stephanie journaled and meditated every day, and had even started mentoring in the meta-physical area. She'd also met new friends and I have to admit I was a bit jealous.

Stephanie knew I was intuitive and she encouraged me to dig into it, and though I was really skeptical I agreed to attend an expo with her. I didn't have a reading that day but I did have reflexology done and purchased a few crystals. I also attended her 50th birthday party and a couple people mentioned my psychic abilities. I stepped in and out of the realm several times.

After a couple of other expos and some private readings, I felt the need to look into this further. I read a couple of books on psychic abilities and did a couple of sessions with Stephanie's mentor. I also took classes in subjects such as intuition, archangels, and guardian angels, taught by leaders at the top of the field. I had finally let go of resistance and decided it was time to learn everything I could.

I began to re-examine my childhood and realized that I had always been gifted with claircognizance, or clear knowing. I even remembered being called a "know-it-all" in school and by a few relatives.

Not everyone is a claircognizant; however, there are five other intuitive "clairs."

1. **Clairvoyance** is visual, meaning seeing signs from spirit through the Third Eye. Common signs are:
   - Seeing images in a dream.

- Experiencing "déjà vu." The feeling that you have been somewhere or done something before.
- Finding coins on the ground. This is a loved one sending you their love and support.
- Seeing butterflies and dragonflies. These are signs of spiritual rebirth, creativity, endless potential and change.
- Finding feathers. Feathers are also a sign from deceased loved ones who want you to know they are around.

Not long after my dad passed away our family went out to dinner. When the waitress brought chicken fried steak with milk gravy, we looked at each other and smiled. None of us had ordered it but it was a favorite of Dad's. There was no doubt he was with us that night.

2. **Clairaudience** – Hearing.
   - Sounds
   - That small inner voice you hear
   - A song on the radio
   - Ringing in your ears
   - Whispers behind you when there is no one there

I was driving in my car and heard a song that I had not listened to since college. The following weekend my son and I attended a football game. During the game one of my college friends reached out and met up with me and my son at half-time.

3. **Clairsentience** – Feeling the presence of Spirit, physically or emotionally.
   - Chills or goosebumps

- A gut feeling
- Heavy heart (If feeling physical pain, get checked out by a physician. You may actually be dealing with a medical issue.)
- A brush of wind against your face

We've all heard stories about a mother having a deep feeling that something has happened to one of her children, only to find out that the child was in an accident.

4. **Clairfragrance** (also called clairalience or clairolfactance) – Psychic smell.
   - Perfume
   - Baked goods
   - Flowers

Have you ever smelled the bread that Grandma used to bake or aftershave that Dad used?

5. Clairgustance – Receive message from Spirit by taste.
   - Did your Grandpa smoke? Can you taste the tabaco in your mouth? That is Grandpa letting you know he is there.
   - My Grandma put on so much of her Lavender perfume I swear I could taste it. I know who's around if I taste it now.

Everyone is born with the ability to communicate with Spirit (Intuition). Some people have stronger abilities than others. That doesn't mean your intuition can't be developed over time. It just takes practice and trust.

Here are some fun ways to practice.

The Reading Minds Game

This is a great one to do with a friend. Decide on a subject; for this example we will use animals. Ask your partner to think of one animal in their head. Let yourself relax for a few minutes and then say out loud what animal comes to mind. Notice how much better you get with more and more practice. The more you practice, the more comfortable you are, and the more you trust your first gut feeling.

The Card Experiment

Use a deck of playing cards. Shuffle and pick one card out. Make sure it is upside down so you can't see it. Once you feel like you know what the card is turn it over and see if you are right. If you don't get it right the first time don't get discouraged. You can also do this with a partner.

Tune into Someone and Guess How They are Feeling

Start your morning by guessing what kind of mood your family, boss or coworkers will be in. Or, let your intuition tell you (through pictures in your mind, thoughts in your head, or a feeling in pit of your stomach) how your spouse or children will be acting at the end of the day (providing they are not always crabby – ha ha).

Practice Automatic Writing

Quiet your mind by meditating for five to ten minutes, then sit down with a pen and piece of paper. Think about something you'd like guidance on, then soften your hand. Try not to think too much and let go. The more you do this, the better you will get at it. Your intuition will be flowing through your hand onto the paper. This will amaze you.

And My Personal Favorite...

Take a box of recipe cards. On one side write words, shapes, letters or anything you would like. Turn them face down and intuit what is on the card. Take this game with you when you are traveling.

You can also intuit the first animal you will see, what color the first person you see has on, the first vehicle you will pass, and so on. Use your imagination.

For all of the practices, keep track of the wins.

After forty years in the corporate world, I now have a business reading Oracle Cards and providing Reiki Energy Healing, with plans to grow into other spiritual/intuitive areas, including teaching. How I wish I had taken an interest sooner and talked with Aunt Grace and learned from her! She was an original in more ways than one. I do know that I am finally doing my life's work and I wouldn't want to be anywhere else. Pay attention, look, listen, feel, smell and know. Where is your intuition? It is there.

Cindy Merriam is a Spiritual Intuitive, certified Oracle and Tarot Card Intuitive, Reiki Practitioner, certified Mind, Body and Spirit Practitioner, and owner of Reflections with Cindy. Before starting her business, she spent thirty-five-years in corporate America, where she negotiated millions of dollars in transportation savings and led corporations to reduce their carrier base while obtaining excellent pickup and delivery service.

It is her love for spiritual work that led her to contribute to *The Wild Women's Book of Shadows*. It is her first published work, but certainly not her last.

Cindy is from Superior, Wisconsin and a graduate of the University of Wisconsin-Superior. She currently resides in Coon Rapids, Minnesota with her husband and son, both named John. Cindy and her son are both avid fans of the Green Bay Packers. John and his dad frequently attend the Minnesota Golden Gopher Hockey Games.

www.reflectionswithcindy.net

reflectionswithcindy@gmail.com

THE MAGIC OF BEES

Erin Christine

It was March of 2002 and I was sitting across from a tiny, ethereal woman named Jenny. She had delicate features and blond hair down past her waist. She said she was an angel reader, but I'll be darned if she didn't look just like an angel herself! I spent an hour with her while she relayed things to me from the angelic realm. Some of her words resonated deeply inside my being, while others just seemed too much for me to believe.

At one point during the session, she said to me, "You have faeries flying all around you!" She then went on to tell me that faeries are angelic messengers that watch over the planet and all her elements. They are the keepers of our land, bodies of water, plant life, animal life – basically anything in the natural world is protected and nurtured by the faery realm. And because I was very pregnant at the time, she mentioned that the faery realm also watched over the children of this world. Jenny then gave me a list of books and meditation CDs to help me learn how to connect with the angels and faeries on my own. I really didn't know what to think of this woman and all she had shared with me, but I floated out of her office feeling strangely euphoric and dreamy.

One week later I was sitting on the patio in my backyard, headphones on, ready to embark on my very first guided meditation experience. I had no expectations, but I was overthinking everything! I closed my eyes and just let myself listen to the soothing voice and curious words. I surprised myself by falling into a deeply relaxed state. When the meditation ended, I sat there for a long moment just breathing in the bliss I felt. This was a new feeling for me!

I opened my eyes and stared into my backyard. It looked cloudy and alive, almost like a wave of water was washing over the entire yard and I could see through it to the other side. It felt like several minutes had passed as I just stared off into space. I had never felt this at peace before, and that's when it happened! It was as if someone had taken a large orange Home Depot bucket filled with gold glitter and threw it right at my face. Gold flecks filled the air, and I didn't dare breathe. I just stared, wide-eyed, watching them flutter around me. Suddenly, they showed themselves. The flittering gold began to take shape until I saw tiny, iridescent bodies with shimmery wings surrounding me. What on earth was happening? Was I really seeing what I thought I was seeing? If I closed my eyes, would they still be there when I opened them? I didn't want this beautiful magic to end, but I had to know. So, for one long moment, I squeezed my eyes shut. I took in a deep breath and opened them again. The shimmering figures remained. I didn't know it in that moment, but I had just met my spirit guides.

It has been nearly two decades since this experience. My guides have been ever-present, active participants in my life. They've taught me the language of nature, the ebb and flow of change, and how to connect deeply with all of life. Sharing this message with you is my promise to them, my gift back to God, to help protect and honor Mother Earth. In the pages that follow, I am going to take you on a magical journey into some of the deepest parts of nature and share with you a radical method of meditation that has changed my life in unimaginable ways. It is my hope that after reading this you will have the courage to face your greatest fears, acquaint yourself with your true nature, and build and/or strengthen your relationship with Mother Earth.

What if you sat down one day, closed your eyes, and suddenly saw yourself looking out through the eyes of a bee? What if, next thing you know, you're flying through the air, gliding in and out of plants and flowers. You can see all the parts up close – the veins in each leaf, the stems, the beautiful bounty of photosynthesis at work. It's a fantastic feast for your senses. You are the bee, but you are still you as well! As you journey along you are gathering information, expanding your vision, and moving through a space that you could have never imagined. Think it sounds crazy? Well, it's exactly what happened to me in the spring of 2017.

Bees had been following me around for years, loudly interrupting my hikes, landing on my pen while I journaled outside, coming into my house and, on more than one occasion, literally flying beside my car as I drove down the road. I found them frustrating and annoying – quite frankly, a pain in my butt. I just wanted them to leave me alone. It wasn't until after my experience that I realized they were trying to get my attention, and it was time to listen.

I still remember the day one came into my house. I was anxiously trying to get him outside without harming him or getting stung in the process. And in that moment, when I was so freaked out, I suddenly heard very clearly in my mind, "Why are you running away from yourself?" Something in those words hit down to my bones. From that day on, every time a bee invaded my space, I would be still and listen. Don't get me wrong, though, I resisted like crazy! I had never been stung and I certainly didn't want to start now. But even deeper than that was an incredible fear that surged through my being. It felt paralyzing. Have you ever felt this fear? Where does it come from? Why is it so overpowering? These questions and so many others rolled through my mind. The only way I was going to find out was to welcome the fear and sit with the bees.

I started with baby steps. I made wonder and curiosity my new best friends and just showed up. I believe this step alone was the most powerful and created the most momentum in my quest. I quickly learned that the more I sat still and listened, the less fear I felt. Are you willing to show up for yourself and find out what the bees want to share with you? Let's get started then!

Step 1-Invitation/Visualization

Inviting the bees into your world is a very brave first step. This can be done at night before sleep, to have them enter your dreams. If this is the way that feels best to you, keep a journal and pen close by to make note of your dreams immediately upon waking, even before you get out of bed. You can also invite them anytime during the day, wherever you are. Bees are diligent messengers of the natural world. They will hear you no matter where you are and what words you use; they will even hear you through your fear and doubt. Bees are attracted to a pure and gentle heart, you need only approach with sincerity and kindness. Visualizing a single bee or group of bees is also a great way to connect with their energy. This can be done simultaneously with the invitation process. You'll need to find a quiet space to sit or lay down. Close your eyes, take in a few slow, deep breaths, and visualize your bee guides.

In either of these methods, you can have a question ready that you would like to have them answer or you can just ask them what message they have for you. We live in a loud, busy world. Communicating with the natural world requires immense patience and trust if its new to you. It also requires consistent practice. Make it a point to connect with your bees daily, even if just for a few minutes. I've found that telepathy is their primary means of relaying information to you. It may sound like your own thoughts in the beginning, but the more times you reach out to them, the better you'll be able to distinguish their voice from your own. Some of the ways that messages come through for me is through specific song lyrics suddenly playing over and over in my head (especially songs I've not heard in years), movie quotes, billboards, license plates, or even straight-up voices speaking out of the blue. I even hear different languages and accents from time to time. Over time, you will build a strong rapport with your guides and you will know without a doubt what they are trying to say to you. Once you feel at ease here, move on to step 2.

Step 2-Sitting at a window and watching them work

You'll need to find a quiet space, this time in front of a window looking directly out at a tree or bush where bees hang out during the day. Pull up a comfortable chair and get as close to the window as possible. The idea here is to really see the bees and how they operate. Getting a closer look allows you to see the life inside of them and how they show up for humanity. There is much to learn from bees and the more we see them for their magic, the more we can honor them as an integral part of this world. So, just as you did in step 1, sit quietly, eyes open this time, take in a few deep breaths, and have your question ready. Again, when you feel ready, move on to step 3.

Step 3-Sitting outside directly front/center of their favorite tree or bush

Note: Working with bees is about honoring space. If you are allergic, please honor yourself and stick to the first 2 steps. If you really want to stare your fears down, choose another insect. This method can be done with any bug or animal that calls to you.

I have a robust, red lantana bush in front of my house that is packed with bees daily. I sit on the walkway in front of it, with bees flitting less than an inch from my face. While you do not have to sit with them this close to you, do choose a location that allows you to get as close as possible. You may need a yoga mat or pillow for comfort. This position can be triggering, so be patient with yourself. Take slow, deep breaths to calm and center. You may notice your heart racing. You may feel the urge to run or swat them away. Sit with this discomfort. Just sit with it. Stillness and willingness to look beyond the fear make miracles happen.

Some questions to consider while sitting with the bees:

- What are your greatest fears?
- Where does pain show up in your world?
- In what ways do you feel small and insignificant?
- Where in your life are you out of balance?
- What distractions keep you from taking action on your dreams?
- What one small thing can you do today to make this world a better place?
- Are you willing to turn that one thing into a daily practice for even greater impact in the world?

I have spent countless hours in meditation and various forms of communication with the spirit world. But connecting directly with bees has been the most magical experience of my life. It has changed me in beautiful and profound ways. It has the power to change you too! Bees are here to teach us how to become one with our purpose. They ask us to claim our most potent self, breathe life into our gifts, and come out of hiding.

Who would you "bee" without your fear? Are you ready to find out?

Erin Christine has spent a lifetime trying to make sense of a world she could not fit into. A storyteller, seer, poet and magician, Erin weaves her own world, breathing in a balance of human suffering and alchemy. She sees beyond the veil and feels the world's pain. This gift has granted her access to the deepest parts of herself and has led her to her sacred work.

Erin Christine is a Certified Transformational Life Coach, Licensed Massage Therapist specializing in Reflexology and Toe Reading, and a Reiki Master/Teacher. For almost two decades, Erin has traveled within and around the spirit realms navigating life as a clairvoyant, clairaudient and empath. Her connection to the spirit and natural worlds allows her to take a shamanic approach to her sessions, creating space for her clients to access their own healing. Her gentle bodywork and dialogue techniques help her clients tune into the stories and wounds living inside their bodies that are ready to be healed.

Erin tries her best to live a normal life in Phoenix, Arizona with her daughter, Savannah Faith. It is her lifelong dream to be a bestselling author.

www.erinchristine.org

FINDING MAGIC
Esme Chamane

"I know I am growing when I can bend,

when the wind blows, survive the rains,

and still reach for the sun."

~ Esme Chamane, age 14

Heart Lessons

"The greatest thing you will ever learn, is just to love and be
loved in return."

~ Eden Ahbez

Throughout my life my heart has provided me with lessons
that guided me on the path to discovering magic; they
taught me where to step, where to step away. I thank Spirit
for every love, every heartbreak along the way to finding my

power. Every wound healed in time and created a heart opening, a portal for wisdom. My heart opened slowly as I began to understand myself and others with compassion. Forgiveness followed – healing, freeing, leaving my heart open to receive more love. I thank Spirit for my mistakes and losses because in the end they taught me how to love deeply. And love taught me magic.

Magic is not just a belief that unseen, mystical forces are at work, it is a warm *knowing*. It happens when your soul knows that a power greater than your own is present. To discern it is a gift. To channel it is an even greater gift. It was through my love for my parents that I recognized I had the gift of mediumship, and became aware of magic throughout my life.

The Path to Magic

One mediumship class exercise revealed a thread of magical occurrences in my life. The teacher asked me to examine what senses I use to do a reading, and in what order. I tend to feel, then see. Suddenly a litany of memories, from long before I studied spirituality, came back to me, providing evidence that swept away all my doubts.

If my childhood experiences of playing with a Ouija board, levitating with friends, and reading books about Edgar Cayce planted seeds, I cannot say. I do know, however, that attending parochial schools validated my belief in magic. I first found magic in chapels. Lit candles, stained glass, statues were mystical. The priest, chanting and wafting incense, myrrh, as he walked up to the altar, connected me to the power of the Unseen. As a child, I "felt" when a chapel was filled with prayer.

There were many times, more than I can list, when I dismissed what was occurring at the time. Now I recognize that I was finding magic.

Here are the most salient memories that surfaced:

- I had a vivid dream of an angel, in a rich flowing burgundy garment, purposely flying through the air in slow motion. Her arms were slowly moving with lightning flashes of sparkling pure light instead of wings. As her arms moved in flight, there was a silence that felt as powerful as a deafening sound. *I felt the sound.* It was beautiful.

- I was walking down a hall at work on May 25, 1979 when I felt an energy plunge. I later learned that Flight 191 had crashed at Chicago O'Hare Airport at that exact time, killing 277 passengers.

- I dreamt there was a national disaster. I was in New York and there was debris falling from the sky. I looked up and there were two plumes of smoke in the sky. The next day, the Columbia shuttle crashed. I saw the exact two plumes of smoke on the news that evening.

- I toured a medical school prior to attending. The first time I saw a cadaver in the morgue, I knew the soul existed. It was so clear there was that the life force that had animated the body was now absent.

- I had an on-and-off boyfriend who was a doctor where I worked. One day, while we were in "off "mode, I felt the sensation of sand under my feet as I walked through the parking lot. Later I found out he was on vacation with someone else.

- While in business school, I had a dream I was wading through mud to get to an island of pink flamingos. The next day my calculus professor said, "Let's say you had pink flamingoes and wheelbarrows of mud..." as he reached to describe quantities.

- I mindlessly doodled a little dog quite often, only to realize, after adopting a dog, that it was him! Sammy was my soulmate dog. I traveled everywhere with Sammy, including a resort in Santa Barbara. Years after he passed, my husband and I stayed at the same resort. While there, I asked Sam for a sign that he was okay. In our room was a travel magazine with an article called "Travels with Sam: A Man and His Dog Explore Santa Barbara" – just as I once did with Sammy!

I realized Spirit had been active in my life all along!

You may recognize that once you begin a spiritual journey, there is no going back. While you cannot unlearn what has warmed your soul, you can let go of the things that do not fit your soul's purpose. Other things will empower you and lead you to further self-discoveries. That is the first step to finding your magic: notice your strengths. This is how mediumship opened up to me.

Heaven Opened

Out beyond ideas of wrong doing and right doing, there is a field. I'll meet you there.

When the soul lies down in that grass,

The world is too full to talk about.

Ideas, language, even the phrase each other

doesn't make any sense.

~ Rumi

After my parents passed – first my father then my mother a few years later – I received clear messages from them. It began with psychic messages, followed by messages from the other side.

My father, Jimmy, had rural roots and a metropolitan worldview, and he spent the last years of his life in an assisted living facility in Chicago. It resembled a country club, and in fact he told me that prior to living there he'd had a dream of moving into a country club.

I treasured our conversations, especially because I knew our days were numbered. One morning as I woke up, I dreamt I was standing in the woods looking up at trees with sunlight flickering through their leaves. That evening, I spoke to Jimmy, just checking in, listening as he recounted his day. As we were saying goodbye, he asked, "Have you ever seen the leaves flickering in sunlight?"

Two days after my father passed away, I was awakened in the middle of the night by the feeling that my right toe had been pinched. I immediately sensed it was Jimmy's spirit. I woke my husband up to tell him, half asleep, he understandably had no comment. The next day, when I went to Jimmy's apartment to pack up his things, I noticed one of the legs on a wooden chair was broken. This caught my attention because Jimmy had been unable to walk. Then Patrick, the angel of a man from Ghana who had cared for Jimmy, stopped by. When I shared I my pinched toe experience with Patrick, a warm broad smile came over his face. He told me he used to wake my father by pinching his toe. My father's dementia at the end caused him to be confused during sundown and awakening, so pinching helped. Patrick said *his* toe had been pinched three times since my father's passing! When it first happened, he'd thought, *That is "Daddy"* – a term of affection he used for Jimmy.

Both of my parents gave their bodies to medical schools, and after my mother passed her ashes were not due to arrive for one to two years. Imagine my surprise when they came in just ten months, and the Friday before Mother's Day. When I reached for the phone to call my husband, my mother's photo was suddenly my phone's screensaver! I had no logical explanation for this, and when I used the phone again it had changed back.

The following month I visited Denise Linn's ranch in California to receive my Soul Coaching certification. I was missing my parents, and the rolling land at the ranch reminded me of the beautiful land they had lived on in Maryland. Two different times during that stay I reached for my phone and my mother again showed up as the screensaver! I recognized it as a sign of her love and that I was on the right path.

The communication I lovingly received from my parents in spirit led me to help others connect to loved ones. The magic continued as I developed the gift of mediumship. When I make a connection a warm chill travels down my back, often continuing down my legs. It is the most loving exhilarating energy, as if the loved ones are thanking me for delivering their message.

On my spiritual path I've had many spiritual teachers – some famous, some not, some animals, all profound. One famous medium advised me to "go to the love to make a connection." This has always been my guiding light. I now create an opening to receive the love connection departed souls have with my sitter. The emotion of love is the most powerful to tap into. Love never dies.

Tapping into the Power of the Unseen

Creating Sacred Space for Spiritual Work

Rooms have energy. Clean and de-clutter the space with the intention of releasing the old and bringing in the new. De-cluttering is also an act of forgiveness.

Be mindful of all your senses as you prepare sacred space.

- Visuals should be safe and beautiful, with relaxing colors and sacred images.
- Sound is a connection to the fifth dimension; for example, music, drums, rattles, bells.
- Smells provide evidence of the unseen. Incense has been used in ceremonies throughout time to symbolize our connection with Source, for example, sage, cedar, sweetgrass, fire.
- Touch is a symbol of physical awakening. Soft textures create ease and the sensation of all the footsteps of our lifetime on Earth.
- Taste nurtures our body. Drink water with cinnamon stick, sliced apple.
- Table Placement of the four Elements:
    o Air Feather – East
    o Water Seashell –West
    o Earth Crystals – North
    o Fire White Candle – South
- Light a white candle with intention and use it to burn sage, moving the sage clockwise three times. Place your hand on your heart and allow your heart to fill with Love and Light. Breathe in knowing, breathe out doubt. Breathe in love, Breathe out fear.

- Burn sweetgrass from the same candle and call in angels, guides, and loved ones in spirit.
- Use your intuition to select crystals, cards, or to just open to any guidance.

Invocations

The following rhymes came easily to me, though at first I thought I was just creating affirmations. Now I recognize the power of these words. For example, "Expedite" created a result as I wrote it! The same day it was written, I received a phone call that provided a down payment on our new home without tapping our savings.

Words also become more powerful with repetition, so I invite you to embrace and vocalize whatever calls you.

Invocation before a Reading

Thank you, Spirit, for making me a channel of Light, Wisdom, and Love.

I open to messages from Above.

Now to speak soft and clear,

To bring our Angels and loved ones near.

Surrounded in your Love we send

Thanks to you without end.

So be it, and so it is.

Expedite

Coming now through Time and Space

The wish is granted without wait

For the greatest good of all

We release our Call

So be it, and so it is.

Solution

As water flows freely through the stones

Prayer is answered through all obstacles shown

Swiftly flying and landing near

We find the answer we seek so dear

Thank you, Mother/Father God.

Peace and Courage

Divine Mother/Father see us through

In our hour of need we call to you

Help us to see Your Good Grace

In the situation we now face

Help us to find Peace in our Hearts

No matter what darkness starts

Our Light will shine as we reach to You

And you reach back through all we do.

And so it is.

Close sessions with gratitude and a singing bowl. Wash your hands with cold water at the close of psychic or mediumship sessions to cut energy.

From my heart to yours I invite you to walk your path as Archangel Uriel holds the lamp for your discernment, Archangel Michael leads you safely, Archangel Gabriel walks behind you to whisper good and Archangel Raphael heals you every step of the way.

Walk in Beauty. Find your magic.

It is the journey, not the destination.

Esme Chamane, a pen name, means "Beloved Shaman." Esme is a spiritual counselor, Soul Coach, speaker, writer, and Reiki Master Teacher practitioner. She has held many workshops at Unity Church. Her website is www.home4thesoul.com.

THE WILD SEEKER:
STUCK BETWEEN TWO WORLDS
GG Rush

"I am fulfilled when I can be who I want to be."

~ Deepak Chopra

I am a seeker. A student who constantly craves knowledge. I have studied Reiki, meditation, tarot, herbalism, aromatherapy, Wicca, tapping, belly dancing and crystal healing. Over the last year I took my first art class since high school and painted the goddess Green Tara. I was surprised by how good it came out and how much I enjoyed painting. And that is just the beginning. I plan to continue learning and I imagine I will one day incorporate these things into my practice as a healer. But what led me to this quest? Why do I continue to spend money on class after class, lecture after lecture? Why do I seek something called Enlightenment? A recent epiphany finally answered these questions, and I share it with you here in the hopes that it will help to inspire your own shift.

My journey began with Reiki. Marina, my Reiki Master, opened my mind to the possibilities that existed outside of my "normal" life. By normal I mean my day-to-day as a divorced mother, bookkeeper, and Girl Scout Cookie mom. At the time I was afraid, broke and alone and knew I needed to change things. First, I studied how to save money and budget, and once my finances were on solid ground I started to travel and see the world. I attended a few seminars and noticed I was filled with yearning; I was starting to imagine another life for myself. At a seminar in Phoenix I remember standing in front of the stage in an empty conference room and longing to be on it. I even took a picture of myself to keep as a reminder. Then, while studying under my mentor in Africa I learned I wanted to be a life coach and build my resume as a healer. I started studying harder, and found that no matter how many classes or seminars I took there was always another fascinating one around the corner, with teachers that were accessible and passionate about sharing what they knew. I followed and listened and learned all I could, but that question was always in the back of my mind: Where am I going?

That trip to Phoenix marked a major turning point in my journey. I met and connected with a woman who was a publisher – the first I had ever met. She saw something in me and asked me to join a compilation book she was putting together. My submission was about my observations of a lion pride while on a silent game drive in Africa. How incredible it felt to see my words in print! From there I went on to be a contributor to five more compilation books. My publisher asked me to write about my solo travels, and that book will be published later this year. My journey as a writer has happened so organically that I started to believe in myself and explore other options to get me to where I really want to be … which leads me to my recent epiphany.

During a Reiki session with Marina I realized that I was living a double life. I have a boring day job that pays my bills and provides medical insurance, and more importantly, funds my "other life" – my travels, my classes, my seeking. But living this double life is also exhausting. Each day at work I feel like I am an actor playing a part. It stifles me and drains my creativity and makes me feel unfulfilled. It makes me think I will continue to remain stuck and unfulfilled, constantly longing to explore, experience and express myself fully. I am afraid I will disappear into this world where I don't really belong.

Once the workday is finally over, I am finally able to live my true calling – doing the things that feel authentic to me and feeling happy and of service to the Universe. When I write, paint or take classes, I feel alive. Like I course-corrected my trajectory. Picking up a pencil, holding a crystal, and mediating all make me feel I am answering the call to be my true self.

Once I recognized the disconnect between my two lives, it became easier to envision the path to being my true self. More than envisioning it, I realized I was already on that path. When I am in that space, I know I am exactly where I belong. When I surrender to the Universe, when I am curious about learning more, when I am in this Sacred Place, I know my acceptance and faith in myself is growing. I am evolving every day.

Here are the daily rituals that keep me walking this path to my true self:

Morning Ritual

Every morning before I get out of bed I do a two-minute gratitude meditation. Then, after pouring myself a cup of coffee and feeding my cat Bella, I light some palo santo and put on music, usually Deva Premal. Now I am ready to pull oracle cards from my many decks. I look for inspiration and intention for my day ahead. I read from a daybook of inspirational ideas, then I then pull out a journal and write something I am grateful for. It can be anything from "I am grateful it's Friday" to "I am grateful for all that I will learn today." I then do a deeper meditation – twenty to thirty minutes. I can then go to work calm, grounded and prepared for that day. Best of all, I always feel I have already accomplished something meaningful.

Evening Ritual

When I come home from work I spend thirty minutes in meditation, preferably out on my back porch if the weather permits. I then go for a walk or ride my stationary bike. I usually spend another hour in creative play – writing, drawing, painting or coloring. I love to cook so I prepare something healthy and wonderfully tasty to nourish my body. And before I go to bed I reflect on my day and what I accomplished, knowing that I took the time to fill my body and soul with that which my heart craves. No matter what happened during the day at work I feel a sense of peace and gratitude.

On Saturdays I take ballroom dance – something I never thought I would or could. Boy, was I was wrong! I have been in three showcases doing the rumba, foxtrot and waltz. Now I am learning tango. A person with no natural rhythm is dancing quite well. This is how I work toward my goal of living my life authentically – one step at a time. Will I just up and quit my day job? Probably not yet, but I am laying the groundwork. This is the thrill of seeking. This is the feeling of being a Wild Women. Because I know that the life I crave is attainable and real. I will get there, and putting this in words on a page is part of that process.

Whether you know it or not, you too have a Wild Woman inside you, seeking the freedom to be true and authentic creature you were meant to be. To be brave enough to claim your place and live your life in sacred grace. To join the Wild Women Tribe – vibrantly alive!

May reading this be the first step of your journey.

Namaste.

"I would love my older self to not be in the story of how it should have been, but to live in deep acceptance of how it is."

~ Boyd Varty

Gail "GG" Rush Gould is a perpetual student and seeker of knowledge, experience and enlightenment. She is certified Reiki II and is studying Reiki III under Master Marina Lando, MS, who has also taught her Aromatherapy, Chakra Balancing, Toxic Emotions and the ancient art of Pulse Reading. GG is also a "Wayfinder Life Coach In-Training" and attended Martha Beck's African Star Program at Londolozi Game Reserve in South Africa. In addition to her solo travels around the world she is currently working on a book about her journeys and self-discovery, due out later this year. GG resides in Cary, North Carolina with her cat Bella.

THE TRANSFORMATIVE POWER OF NATURE

Ghene't Lee-Yong

There once was a child who loved the outdoors. She climbed trees, dug in the dirt, ran through grass, chalked on the sidewalk, and walked for hours under the heavy gaze of the southern sun. Time would stand still as she lay in the grass, watching the clouds drift by above. Her mind wandered and worlds were created in that standing time. That child was me and I was that child. Then, something happened. I do not know when it happened, but it did nonetheless. I lost that love and in fact forgot I ever had it.

For years I dreaded the outdoors. The heat, the harshness of the sun, the insects, and the mess of it all, I found distasteful. Distasteful to the point of aversion. If I went out it was to get from my house to my car or from my car to some other building. The one exception was when my children were babies. I would take them for walks in their strollers at night. We would look for planets, stars, and satellites.

During my disconnect from nature I also suffered a disconnect from myself. I was in a very unhealthy marriage. I suffered from codependency and enabled and allowed unacceptable behavior. Some days I felt as if I were mad. I was emotionally, physically, and spiritually distorted. Emotionally, I was angry, sad, or scared – sometimes all three. Spiritually, I knew there was a power greater than myself but could not know that It concerned Itself with me. Physically, I was always sick. I was fifty pounds overweight and suffered from severe stomach pains, respiratory illnesses, and leg pains.

I knew not who I was.

Yet, this state served a purpose. My unhappiness helped me to see the need for change, and I latched on to the one thing I could control: my weight. And this realization brought me back to nature. Hiking, walking, and swimming were outdoor activities that helped me literally get outside of my circumstances. As I spent time in physical activity outdoors I began to release weight, gain strength, and rediscover my love of nature. Through this re-discovery, through this new adventure in nature, I found something I had no idea I was looking for, something I had no idea could be mine. That something was connection.

Being in nature connected me to that which is greater than myself. It gave me time to listen, to think, to cry, and to voice my frustrations and fears out loud, in a safe space, where only Source could hear me. And in that alone-but-not-alone space I could also listen to what guidance Source had to offer. It did not come in words, per say, though sometimes I did hear words, brief snatches of a phrase. Mostly, however, it worked by energetically shaping my thoughts, and even the formation of those thoughts. As I walked trails and woodland paths that were new to me, my brain worked to keep up with and receive the input. It created new neural connections that opened up new ways for me to process information of all kinds and gently guided me to the answers and solutions – pathways I needed to take in my everyday life and find my way out of the darkness.

Eventually, as I healed my physical distortion, I began to heal my emotional and spiritual distortion as well. Not only did I lose weight; I also moved our family out of a neighborhood I was not comfortable in to a nicer one closer to work and school. I then applied for and was hired at a job that provided more income and long-term stability, which was a great help when my marriage ended and I found myself a single mother of two.

Having achieved such a wonderful outcome, I began thinking about how I could share it with others. My reconnection with nature had transformed me mind, body, and spirit, and I just knew it could do the same for anyone seeking another way to live. I began hosting hiking tours to get individuals and families outdoors and exploring places they would not explore on their own. It did not matter if these were local areas; all that mattered was that they walked outside their comfort zone, that they took a step into the unknown and trusted.

In working with many I have found that it is not easy in our modern world to trust nature. To walk into the woods alone, to pass by animals of all shapes and sizes, and to hold to the path until the trail is complete takes courage. The elements are what they are and they do not bend to the will of man. It is up to us to find that flexibility within ourselves. In order to connect with nature one must indeed connect *with* nature. Touch it. Hold it. Be held by it.

The following are three techniques that I use personally and that those who work with me find the most powerful. You may do them in one session or choose to do each on a separate occasion. The more often you use them the more in depth and transformative the experience. Everyone will have a different experience, and each experience will be different.

Establishing Connection

Choose an outdoor space you want to explore. This could be a trail, a spot by a lake or river, or the ocean. Take a few minutes to observe your surroundings. Note the temperature, the colors, the smells, the sounds. Breathe deeply and ask, silently or out loud, "What object shall be my guide today?" Observe your surroundings again. You may be drawn to a stick or rock. It may be a shell or log. Whatever it is, approach and hold the object the best way you can. Remember that all things are from one Source, the grand architect of our universe. I know this source as God. Ask God what message is intended for you during this time outdoors.

Wait. Listen. See.

If your object is small enough you may carry it with you as you walk. Be sure to continue observing the environment around you – the light, the trees and leaves. Is the light reflected off the foliage, or absorbed by it? Watch the birds flit from branch to branch or how the surf and the water move over the sand and back out into the ocean again. Pay attention to how you feel. Are you tired? Are you calm? Is happiness present, or sadness? What thoughts come and go as you travel through this natural space? You may choose to bring a pen and paper to journal about your experience, or you can pull out your phone and take pictures.

As you head back to your daily life, ask if the object should remain in the environment or if you may bring it with you. Thank God for allowing your time in nature and for the object (even if you are instructed to leave it behind).

Lead with a Question

If there is a matter you need clarity on, set an intention or ask for help in finding the solution that is best for all involved. Then continue your walk or outdoor activity – observing, feeling, and listening.

Express Thankfulness

This is one of the most powerful nature engagements I have experienced. While walking in nature, simply say a phrase of gratitude for as many of the elements as possible. The trees, the branches, the leaves, the soil, the roots, the wind – everything. As you say the words, feel the gratefulness filling your body, mind, and spirit. Let this feeling touch all of you that needs healing, then release that healing back into nature.

It is important to record any ideas, inspirations, or courses of action that come to you. After doing this several times you will begin to see threads of thoughts that will serve as guides for your life. Connection to a higher power is innate in all of us. Nature is a conduit through which we can achieve this connection fully. Through observance of nature we can truly see the care and intention meant for our lives, which in turn moves us to make the best decisions to create the best lives possible.

Ghene't Lee-Yong is a Health and Lifestyle Transformation Coach whose practice focuses on the links among spirituality, nature, and fitness. She has been an outdoor educator for seven years and is certified in Ecotherapy and Wilderness first aid and rescue. Ghene't uses nature immersion, expressive meditation, and targeted exercise and fitness as modalities to unlock unconscious blocks in our life and to awaken us to connection to our inner selves. Recently she was a contestant for the Ms. Health and

Fitness cover contest, in which she placed third in her group. In addition to hiking, Ghene't loves to write, paint, ice skate, dance, and spend time with her two children. Eventually, she will be found in a well-appointed cabin on a forested mountain.

ghenet@strongereveryday1111.com

www.strongereveryday1111.com

HEALING PRACTICES WITH ANCESTRAL OILS

Ginger Parrack

The Wild Woman, in my eyes, is one who has learned or is learning to connect with the Earth Mother on the deepest spiritual level, working on connecting to that inner ancestorial knowledge that is deep within our DNA. We need to reconnect with the old way, the old medicine that our ancestors practiced. The time has come for us to learn that old medicine before it is lost and teach it to our children. When we learn to connect with the plants and their life-giving resources, we have a better understanding of their "medicine."

In herbalism there is a philosophy called the "Doctrine of Signatures" that dates back to the time of Greek physician/ herbalist Dioscorides (40-90 AD). The doctrine states that herbs resemble various parts of the body and can be used to treat those parts. The same goes for food – for example, the pomegranate, as it looks like a heart, has chambers, and "bleeds." Herbalists use it to regulate blood pressure, and it is known for its amazing anti-oxidative effects in the blood.

The same can be said for the plants that produce essential oils. Essential oils are highly concentrated excretions from the plant; they are the natural alchemical synergy between the plant and the sun, and the messengers of the plant's energy and consciousness. When we use the oils we are connecting to the signatures of the plant – the soil in which it grew, the elevation of where it was grown, and the weather it was exposed to – as well as its genus and species.

Science does not yet completely understand the role of essential oils; however, we do know that they are excreted by the plant to attract bees and other insects that will pollinate it and ensure reproduction and survival of the species. We also know that plants excrete their oils in their leaves, bark or through the roots to ward off predators and protect themselves from destruction.

When we buy essential oils to use at home we need to be mindful of where they came from. Science has proven that plants react to their environment in many ways. When you speak to plants they thrive, and plants have been recorded moving to music. The essential oils from flowers, leaves, stems and roots have a psychological and spiritual resonance. I truly believe how they are gathered, processed and sold affects the energy of the essential oil.

Native Americans have always been conscious of this. In the Southwest, when they gather plants for medicine or for a particular use such as soap or food, they are careful not to take from the mother plant or take too much of the plant so as to ensure survival and regrowth. They also ask the plant's permission to take it and leave an offering of tobacco or corn in gratitude for its medicine and nutrition.

Unfortunately, given the popularity of essential oils today this practice is not the norm. Plants are gathered quickly; soils are depleted of their nutrients and the distillation is adulterated with whatever else was growing or crawling in the field when the plant of choice was machine-picked. The result: a contaminated essential oil sold just to put money in the manufacturer's pockets, and a plant that was not honored for its medicine and healing properties.

How, you might ask yourself, does this affect the energy of the oil?

When choosing the essential oils for your spiritual work and your medicine, take the time to do your research and find oils that are ethically and organically grown and gathered. They will be more expensive but worth every drop. As you journey through your experience with your connection with the oils and their life source, you will learn to feel the difference in the energy of the oil. You will smell the difference. You will be more discerning in your choices.

Aromatherapy is the use of pure essential oils to improve the mind, body and spirit by application via inhalation or safe topical application to the body. There are so many essential oils that have had a deeply profound effect on myself, my family and many of my clients and/or patients, but there is one that is so deeply spiritual that it must be spoken of and honored most dearly: frankincense, also known as *Boswellia carteri* or Olibanum.

The name frankincense is derived from an old French work *franc,* meaning "free, pure or abundant" and the Latin *incensum,* meaning "to smoke." The Olibanum tree that produces this sacred resin grows in Somalia, Ethiopia and some parts of western India. Frankincense played an important role in ancient Egyptian, Hebrew, Greek and Roman civilizations. Egyptian women charred frankincense and use the back powder, named kohl, to paint on their eyebrows. Frankincense is also referenced in the bible twenty-two times, including as the "gift of the Magi" to baby Jesus, and is considered to be the most important incense since history began.

The tree, which grows between nine and twenty-two feet tall, has thin, narrow leaves and flowers that are white to pale pink in color. The resin is collected by making incisions in the bark; a milky white liquid appears and is allowed to solidify into an orange-brown crystal. It is then steam-distilled or solvent is extracted to obtain the essential oil.

Now let's look at the many uses of frankincense for our health and wellness. Keeping it simple is imperative when using the essential oil, as it affects the nervous system and the muscular skeletal system. It relieves nervous tension and anxiety and relaxes the smooth muscles in the body. As mentioned, there are two recommended ways to experience the oils. One is via inhalation through the nose, whereby the molecules are inhaled into the olfactory system and the bronchioles/lungs, then absorbed through the mucous membranes into the bloodstream. The other method is to apply the oil topically on the skin. (Always keep it away from eyes and make sure to dilute it in a carrier oil or lotion, as many oils can cause irritation and burns to the skin in their concentrated form). There are other practices for the application of essential oils but in my personal opinion those ways are controversial and should only be discussed with a professional aromatherapist or physician.

The energy of frankincense is extremely powerful. As mentioned, the tree has to be cut in order to release its resin or, one could say, the "blood" of the tree. As the tree attempts to heal itself, the wound "scabs" over. This is one energy of the oil: it helps to heal emotional wounds and releases negative energy of that wound. It is also used in "Spiritual Shock" to relax the mind and body so that you can heal from the trauma. Some believe that when the tree is cut the resin comes out in the forms of "tears." Using this oil can relieve us of our emotional pain, the same way we do when we cry.

I used frankincense while working with hospice patients, which opened my eyes to the possibilities of what we can do as family and care providers to assist those who are transitioning from this world to next. As we approach the end of this physical life our body starts to shut down its organs. This change creates elevated levels of waste and chemicals because the liver and kidneys can no longer filter them, and our heart and lungs start to decrease in their normal functions. These changes can cause muscle pain, breathing difficulty and rapid heartrate. Frankincense is known to relieve that pain, and it also relaxes smooth muscles to ease the breathing. I am personally aware of and grateful for the powers of frankincense, for it was the oil I used on my own mother to assist her in her transition to Heaven.

I want to share with you an experience I had with one of my patients (we'll call her Joy) while working at hospice. Joy had a huge loving family and she did not want to leave them. She also had a fear of death and was unsure of her faith in the God of her understanding. We had spoken of this in her final days, and spiritual counseling was provided to her during that time. On the day Joy transitioned her family called and said they were concerned about her; they felt she was struggling and seemed in pain and short of breath. I went to the home, did my assessment and updated the family, and then called the physician. Medications were given per the doctor's orders, but I also offered aromatherapy to assist with her transition. Her family accepted, and I educated them on applying frankincense, blended in an unscented lotion, to the hands and feet. We talked about saying their goodbyes, and I explained to them that the sense of hearing is the first to develop in the womb and the last to go when we transition. Joy would be able to hear them.

Once the family was comfortable with what to do, I left the home. I later learned that Joy passed away peacefully with her loved ones by her side. They were so pleased and comforted that they were able to ease her transition.

Below is the process for you to learn to connect to the essential oils.

Preparing to Connect with Your Essential Oil

- Find a quiet place where you will not be disturbed.

- Have someone choose an oil for you or blindly choose one for yourself. Don't look at the label. Hold the bottle in your hands.

- Have a pen and paper ready to journal your experience.

- Take a few breaths and get comfortable and relax. Take your shoes off and place your feet flat on the floor.

- Close your eyes, take a few more deep breaths, and let go of any issues or concerns.

- Visualize golden light coming into your crown chakra (top of head) and see it going through your body and coming out the bottom of your feet, releasing any negative energy to the earth.

- Open your bottle of the essential oil and place one drop on a tissue or cotton ball.

Connecting with Your Essential Oil

- Remember, don't look at the label on the bottle. You do not need to know the oil. If you do know, release that knowledge and be open to a new experience.

- Smell the oil, using both nostrils at first then plugging off one at a time. This allows the right and left side of the brain to experience the oil. Take your time. There is no need to rush.

Ask yourself these following questions and journal your answers:

- Do you like or dislike the scent? Why?

- How does it make you feel?

- What was the first thought that entered your mind when you smelled this oil?

- Did you have a physical reaction in your body when you smelled this oil?

- What color comes to mind? Do you hear a song or musical note?

- Do you notice a particular place in your body reacting to this oil?

- Does smelling this oil invoke a memory for you? Describe.

- What does this oil smell like to you? (It will not necessarily be the actual plant/flower.)

- Does this oil take you to a place? Do you see pictures when you close your eyes? Describe it if you can.

- If this oil were to give you a message, what would that message be?

- Describe what kind of experience this was for you.

- Continue to sit in quiet and journal your experience with this oil.

My hope is that you find your inner Wild Woman and learn the medicine of the ancestors. Learn about the essential oils, the life blood of the plants, and honor them. The craft must not die with modern ways. There are plants and trees that are becoming extinct and frankincense is one of them. Find ethically and organically grown oils and be open to experiencing the incredible journeys they inspire. Blessings.

Ginger Parrack is a Spiritual Advisor, Clinical Aromatherapist, Psychic/Medium and best-selling author. She came into this world with a knowing and intuition for all that was around her and the ability to see and feel energy. Ginger was born in Phoenix, Arizona, where her family has lived since 1911, and raised in the Sonoran Desert. She has always connected to the energy of the region, along with the ways of the indigenous tribes in the area. Home remedies for healing were a part of her childhood. These healing practices came from the traditions of her ancestors, and they inspired and guided her to go into the medical field. Ginger holds a bachelor's degree in nursing science and has over 200 hours of training in reflexology, auricular therapy and is a reiki master. She has studied Western Herbalism, Flower Essences and healing with crystals and sound. Ginger's passion is to find the balance between Allopathic and Holistic medicine. She is an avid animal lover, amateur photographer and rides her motorcycle to maintain balance in her life.

Website: https://gingerparrack.com

Email: ginger@healingheartmedium.com

Facebook: Ginger Parrack-Healing Heart Medium

Instagram: gingerhealingheartmedium

FROM FEAR TO FABULOUS

Grace Redman

I sat on the sidewalk, crying hysterically. The boy I was dating had just lost his temper over something trivial and exploded in rage, grabbing my car keys from me as I tried to get away and throwing them onto the roof of a nearby office building. He then proceeded to punch me.

The physical pain was nothing compared to the shame, embarrassment and disgust that radiated through my head, soul, and heart. The worst, though, was the paralyzing fear. I felt like laying down and never waking up again.

This was not a new situation. From my teens to my twenties, I consistently attracted abusive toxic interactions – the result of lifelong low self-esteem. I simply didn't feel worthy of love, especially from males. This was all I'd seen growing up – women close to me being emotionally and physically abused by the men in their lives – and that pattern had continued with me, countless times.

I knew in my heart and soul that what I was experiencing was not normal – though many in my circles viewed it this way – but toxic and unhealthy. It also wasn't something I wanted to continue to accept. I knew for damn sure I wanted better for myself.

I started to pay more attention to my small inner voice, the one that whispered quietly to me that there was hope; that I could find a better way. Reflecting back on those dark times, I now know it was God, Source, our Higher Power – whatever you choose to call it –who planted that hope and reason in my mind and pushed me to make a change.

The punch to the head from that boy was my catalyst for change. I couldn't reach out to anyone around me because that wasn't the way we did things in my circle. One didn't speak about emotional challenges; they just sucked it up, put on a happy face and pretended all was perfect. Doing things any other way would be considered "social suicide."

Today, that lost, lonely teenage girl who was in such tre-mendous pain manages one of the most successful staffing firms in the San Francisco Bay Area. I'm also a certified Success and Transformation Coach, working with women to help them break their negative cycles. Perhaps most surprisingly, I've been married to a loving and kind man for over two decades and we have two healthy young adult boys. I've managed to diminish my self-sabotaging behavior. It's taken time, commitment and discipline, plus a firm devotion to self-love and self-care, but I've manifested a fabulous life I LOVE!

I am honored and humbled to be able to share with you what I believe are the most important elements that helped me break generational cycles and rise from victim to victor.

Seek Support and Community

Having a safe space to empty out all of the pain that was eating away at me away and perpetuating my downward spiral was critical.

In the moments following that punch to the head, I had an intuitive flash: I needed professional support and guidance. At nineteen I didn't have much money for a therapist, but through the grace of God I stumbled upon Catholic Charities in my neighborhood. They had a student therapy program and only charged eight dollars a session! I mustered up the courage and called them to make an appointment – the first of MANY.

When I first met Rebekah, a young therapist right out of school, neither one of us could have imagined it would be the beginning of a twenty-five-year relationship! I spent all these years working hard to overcome many challenges, including depression, anxiety, low self-esteem, codependency, a horrible body image and relationship with food, a need to people-please, and workaholism. I learned how to set boundaries, love myself, walk away from toxic situations, and most importantly, find my worth and step into my power!

Rebekah retired a few years ago, and as we sat in our last session together she made a rather surprising admission: the first day we met she'd believed there was no hope for me. She felt I would continue to walk down the same path of abuse, low self-esteem, depression, and anxiety, just like the generations before me. She profusely apologized for thinking this way, saying she was a novice at that time and didn't know any better.

I wasn't offended at all by Rebekah's words. In fact, I felt a tremendous sense of accomplishment. I had broken many unhealthy cycles and manifested and created an incredible life. Granted, it WAS NOT easy, but I did it!

Seeking support and reaching out for help can come in many forms. If traditional therapy isn't available to you, look into the plethora of amazing support groups and communities online. I have been blessed to be part of several incredible groups that have helped me over the years. You can also find individuals who are studying to become therapists and coaches and need clients to practice with – usually at little or no cost. Assess your own social circle and if you have a friend you feel safe with, confide in them. I promise, once you have committed to the intention of seeking support the right opportunity will show up for you.

Study and Learn!

At the tender age of fifteen I stumbled upon Tony Robbins and was fascinated by his thoughts on how to achieve success in life. I listened to everything Tony Robbins, which led me to other great works like Napoleon Hill's *Think and Grow Rich,* Dale Carnegie's *How to Win Friends and Influence People,* and Norman Vincent Peale's *The Power of Positive Thinking.* Later on I discovered spirituality and the Law of Attraction. I have listened thousands of hours of Abraham Hicks and Wayne Dyer, and to this day I spend at least two or three hours every week studying and learning all there is to know about manifesting and creating the life I love. When I began this journey the higher-level concepts would have been way over my head, but the right teacher has always shown up as I was ready to learn the next lesson.

Staying away from mainstream media and immersing myself in information about success and self-development were absolutely necessary for me to retrain my mind and see that I didn't have to live from a victim mentality. All the examples of success I was reading about began to help me create an image of what I wanted my life to look like. We become what we think. We get more of what we focus on. By focusing on and immersing myself in these incredible books I slowly began to create. I don't even think I realized what was happening at the time. I just thought I was reading to gain knowledge. As I look back now I can see how all the studying and learning slowly began to move me from fearful to fabulous.

Gratitude

There is true magic in gratitude; in fact, it is one of the main ingredients to creating a life you love! Even in the most negative of situations we can find things to be grateful for, and when we focus on them we begin to attract more of the same into our lives. I had been conditioned to focus on all the things in my life that weren't going well and then start on the path to fix or make them better. I did create success that way, but let me tell you it was a grind and I found myself burned out many times. However, when I shifted my focus and started practicing gratitude, solutions and opportunities began to present themselves with ease and grace.

Every morning I practice gratitude by writing down ten things that I am grateful for and why. I have fallen off a few times and my life started to go into a state of chaos. Thankfully, the voice of awareness popped up to remind me that I'd lost my focus; I got it back into gratitude and the situation shifted almost immediately. There are many different gratitude journals and practices that you can commit to. I love *The Magic* by Rhonda Byrne, a twenty-eight-day gratitude practice that you can do over and over. It has really changed my life.

Being Out in Nature

The pandemic of 2020 was very challenging in the beginning. The shelter-in-place that we were subjected to created a tremendous amount of grief and loss for me. I was feeling suffocated and at times even my most trusted tools – utilizing my support circle, practicing gratitude, and immersing myself in motivational books and videos – weren't doing the job as well as they used to. Since I couldn't go to the gym I began going outside to get my body moving. Being in nature amongst the trees, water and birds brought me a sense of peace, trust, hope and connection to Source that I had never experienced before. Now I make sure that I get out into nature several times a week to ground myself and connect with my Higher power. Nature reminds me that there is a power so much greater than us, and the vastness of the sky and the ocean validates that abundance is all around us.

Unwavering Faith and Trust

Last but not least, my dear friend, is to have unwavering faith and absolute certainty that you will thrive and create the life you love. You must know without a doubt that you are being guided by a power that is much greater than us all. The Universe does have your back, always. When we trust and have unwavering faith there isn't anything we can't overcome. I have experienced many dark nights of the soul, and as heavy as thing got I knew in my heart that all was going to be well. Time and time again my faith in a Higher Power has never failed me. I allowed myself to sit in the pain with the trust and faith and slowly I would emerge like a butterfly from the chrysalis – wiser, bolder, and more powerful.

We are going to experience tragedy, dark times, and loss; this, my friends, is part of the experience we call life. Just like the dark piece of coal put under tremendous pressure turns into a dazzling diamond, we too will emerge from the most difficult challenges as brilliant beings. The contrast between pain and joy is necessary for us to appreciate the magic of this journey; in fact, I once heard that the depth of joy we experience is equal to the depth of pain we rise out of. I have certainly found that to be true.

I hope my story helps you to realize that no matter our circumstances or background we all have it within us to create and manifest the fabulous life we desire – in fact, it's our birthright to do so. So I say to you: You got this. Go out there and create that life you LOVE!

Grace Redman is an entrepreneur who has owned and managed one of the most successful employment agencies in the San Francisco Bay Area for the last twenty-two years. She is also a Success and Transformation Coach who helps guide others to diminish their negative mental chatter and create a fun and fabulous life they love. Grace holds a master's degree in Organizational Management and is a Certified NLP Master Practitioner, Certified Hypnotist, Certified Reiki Practitioner, and Certified Life Coach. She is a published writer who has contributed to the anthologies *The Kindness Crusader; 365 Days of Self Love; Manifestations;* and *The Grateful Soul,* and regularly shares her tools for growth and empowerment on her podcast, *Real Talk with Grace Redman.*

Grace has a passion for helping people step into their authentic selves and own their power so they can then inspire others and raise the collective vibration. Her services include one-on-one sessions, mentoring packages and VIP days.

Podcast: www.podcasts.apple.com/us/podcast/real-talk-with-grace-redman/id1559065658

Website: www.daretoachieve.com

Facebook: www.facebook.com/grace.s.redman

Email: grace@daretoachieve.com

B.R.E.A.T.H.E.

Heidi Royter

Body ~ Reflection ~ Emotion ~ Attention ~ Tenderness ~
Healing ~Empowerment

For most of my life I felt like I had this gift to leave my body and break away from whatever I was suffering in that moment. As a young girl I would twirl around in the backyard between two tall, full green trees that opened to the clear blue sky, with the sun beaming down upon me. I would spin and weave between the trees, the grass between my toes, until I felt like I was being lifted into the sky and escaping the world. That was the beginning of my journeys to avoid reality. As I grew older, when I did not have the backyard and trees to help me flee, I would just close my eyes and disconnect. Then came the day when I found my breath and reconnected to my body. Since then I have come to realize that the disconnection was for my survival. Today, I still journey and have beautiful experiences, but my breath and body awareness always bring me home to my wholeness and it is a beautiful place to be.

About ten years ago I had reached a place in my life where I was extremely unhealthy. My nervous system was shot, I was removed from myself, and I did not know who I was or understand what had happened to me. Feeling like I had completely lost control of my wellbeing, I committed to a ninety-day journey to heal myself. I knew some of what I would discover would not be "pretty," but it would be the truth. I would also find ways to motivate myself, cleanse myself of self-abuse and redefine myself as a healthy and beautiful woman. Little did I know that this commitment would be much longer than ninety days, or that it would transform my life and heal me on physical, mental and emotional levels. It would also require me to do something I had never consistently done before: stay in my body.

I recall that first morning, opening my eyes and remembering my commitment to focus on me, starting even before my feet hit the floor. As I placed my left hand on my heart and my right hand on my belly (my ritual to stay embodied) I thought I would be focusing on my to-do list for the day, what meals and snacks I would prep, how far I would walk on the treadmill, and how to stay motivated. That is exactly what did *not* happen.

After wriggling around for a moment to get comfortable, I closed my eyes and my attention went to my heart. But I found that I was *uncomfortable* with my eyes closed; my heart felt heavy and there was a part of me inside that did not feel safe. I took in my first breath that I was consciously aware of and it felt so awkward. The inhale through my nose was not deep and the exhale, also through my nose, felt stuffed. My abdomen did not rise. It was like I could barely breathe, which was frustrating to say the least.

I moved on to the second breath, forcing the inhalation and focusing on my belly to push it out, noting that it actually shook as it expanded. Still I continued, counting one breath at a time, toward my goal of ten full breaths. With each breath I became more frustrated; I felt my body resisting and then tears began to surface. By the time I finally reached the tenth breath I wanted to escape, leave my body. This was all too much for me. I did not understand why I was crying. I did not want to cry, yet there I was, unable to stop. I was trying to sort out in my mind why I was feeling this way. Why was the simple act of breathing affecting me so, and how was any of this going to help me? Somehow I knew the only way to get answers to my questions was to continue with the practice each day.

That was a decade ago. As I continued to perform this ritual first thing each morning, I began to have a deeper understanding of my breath and its connection to my body. I learned that allowing myself to honor my feelings is powerful and that I have the right to my experience and to define who I am. I also discovered that being embodied is a gift. I had escaped my body for so long that being outside it felt normal. While this did serve its purpose for survival, full connection to my body is magical.

Breath and Body Scan

Below is a breath and body scan for you to experience being embodied. I recommend having a journal and pen nearby in case you want to write anything down after your experience or make note of areas of your body that had your attention.

Choose a quiet place where you will not have any distractions.

This practice can be done lying down or sitting, whichever you prefer. Make sure you are wearing comfortable clothing.

Some items to consider having available are a blanket to cover yourself, a pillow for under your head and, if lying down, a pillow to place under your knees for additional support.

If you sit in a chair, make sure your feet are flat on the floor and your hands are relaxed in your lap.

Be curious about the physical sensations you feel, and focus on each sensation before moving on to the next. Stay at each site for three complete breaths (an inhalation and exhalation count as one breath). Don't force the breath, but allow it to be natural, smooth and easy. Let go of any story that you have or that arises. You will observe your breath in these areas of the body and observe how the sensation change with the breath.

I invite you to go through the guidelines and then use your breath to scan your body as described.

- Place your left hand on your heart and right hand on your abdomen.

- Notice your breath. Are you breathing heavy, light, rapid, shallow?

- Now bring your attention to your whole body. How does your body feel today? Do you notice any uneasiness or tension anywhere? Do you feel calm or anxious?

- Begin to lengthen your inhalations and full exhalations. Feel your abdomen rising with each inhalation and falling with each exhalation.

- Bring your attention to your heart. Take three breaths, inhaling love and exhaling any sensation weighing on your heart (heaviness, sadness, et cetera).

- If lying down, place your arms down towards your sides, palms facing down for grounding. If you are seated in a chair place your hands on your lap, palms facing down.

- Bring your attention to the tip of your toes and inhale to the crown (top) of your head. Exhale from the crown to the toes for three full breaths.

- Now bring your attention to the bottom of your feet and breathe all the way into them – all ten toes, the tops of your feet and your ankles. Imagine your feet are the gateway to your internal body. They are also the foundation of your entire body, providing support, balance and posture.

- Bring your attention to your legs – the calves, shins, back of your legs, knees, thighs and buttocks. Imagine your breath going into those areas and relaxing them. On the exhale, breathe out any tension. If you lose your focus, just simply bring your attention back to the part of the body that you left off on.

- Now bring your attention to your lower back and abdominal area. Make sure your breathing is smooth, deep and even. Notice whatever you are physically feeling. Focus on an area that is really drawing your attention and notice with each full breath the shifts that take place.

- Move your attention up to the middle of your back, upper back and front of the chest. Notice any tremors in that area and continue to imagine your breath going into those areas and relaxing them. If any thoughts feelings or emotions arise, let them go without attaching to it.

- Turning your concentration to your arms – the whole arm, upper arm, forearm, and that tool of all tools – the hands and all ten fingers.

- Draw attention to your shoulders and neck. If you notice tension in this area after three breaths continue to breathe deeply until it relaxes.

- Now come to your face, relaxing your mouth and jaw and noticing any sensations – hot, cold, tight, or loose. How is this area of your body responding to the breath?

- Move up to your nose, eyes, forehead, and the crown of the head. Be open to receiving whatever you are experiencing. Do not judge what you are feeling; just be neutral, letting any story go.

- Take in a full inhalation at the crown, then completely exhale down to the tip of the toes.

- Lastly, complete three full breaths. As you inhale, scan your whole body, noting the areas in which you feel tension. As you exhale, focus on those areas to relax and release the sensations.

- Slowly bring your attention back to the space you are in. Begin gently wiggling your fingers and toes, rolling your wrists and ankles, and allowing your body any organic movement it is calling for as it reawakens. If you are lying down, roll onto your right- or left-hand side. With your eyes closed, use the strength of your arms to come up to a comfortable seated position. Take a full inhalation and audible exhalation, open your eyes and feel yourself becoming present into the current time and space. Give yourself a few minutes before you get moving.

Here are a few tips to enhance your practice:

1. Practice a ten-minute Breathe and Body Scan in the morning and/or in the evening daily.

2. Use your phone alarm to remind you to take a Breath and Body Scan break two to three times a day.

3. Take a break each hour to breathe for one full minute from your toes to your head, and back down from your head to your toes.

There are many techniques available to calm the mind and relax the body; however, the breath and body scan here are one of the most accessible. You can drop into your body and relax your mind almost immediately, which is why it is also one of the most effective ways to begin a mindfulness meditation. Your body is beautiful and divinely yours; tuning into it gives you control of your journey and allows you to reconnect with physical sensations without judgement or reliving past distressing experiences. Your breath is your lifeforce and your Heaven and Earth connection, so let it do the work to bring you into your wholeness.

Heidi Royter is an Empowerment Coach and the owner of Be Free Wellness and Yoga who assists individuals and groups make changes in their lives and meet their personal and professional goals. She studied Business Management at the University of Nevada, Las Vegas, and certifications as a Mind Body Wellness Practitioner and Clinical Hypnotherapist from the Southwest Institute of Healing Arts. Heidi's approach is nurturing, spirited and direct. She uses breathwork, body scanning, visualization, and holistic nutrition, along with gratitude and appreciation practices with affirmations. In combination, these approaches support the commitment to, and building of, a healthy relationship with self.

Website: http://befreewellnessandyoga.com

Email: heidi@befreewellnessandyoga.com

Facebook: https://www.facebook.com/BeFreeWellnessandYoga

Instagram: https://www.instagram.com/heidi_royter_befree

CREATING BALANCE TO ACHIEVE BLISS

Jill Tyge

They say opposites attract; I believe opposites are here to teach us the biggest lessons in life, such as the need for balance in our mind, body and spirit. Without balance, our lives are out of alignment. I spent many years with people who wanted me to stay silent; they wanted to control what I did, felt, or thought. Sometimes they exercised this control through lies; other times it was through manipulation, game-playing, and threats. I grew up being told to worry about what others thought of me, so I felt like I always had to prove myself. No matter what I did, it was never good enough, and I was ignored or bullied anyway. This created an inner battle within that was very hard to understand. I became more and more insecure and fearful, and though I tried to set boundaries they were not respected. I kept trying to rebuild myself, heal, and move on with the life I wanted and desired, but the sabotage always showed up. I was constantly trying to stay aware and ahead of the next move, and it was slowly suffocating me.

I would hear, "Don't give that energy" or "You are bringing that to yourself," but there was more to it than that. In time I realized that these lessons weren't even mine to learn; I was acting as a mirror for the other person.

It takes time to create balance in ourselves. There is no one class or one teacher that magically solves our problems. It is something we continuously have to work on, just like we do with dieting or exercising. Even when we do keep that balance in check, circumstances can throw us a curveball that makes us stumble and fall into fear and self-doubt. However, with the right tools, we always have the power to bring ourselves back into alignment.

I have spent a lot of my life feeling like I didn't fit in. I would hear things or have this knowing but I didn't know what it was or was told it was my imagination. When I was in the fourth grade my family started going through a lot of trauma that created a stressful household. When I moved out I sought counseling to deal with the impact this stress had on my feelings, behavior and actions. I was asked, "What would you have changed if I could go back?" and even then I said, "Nothing." I knew the circumstance had made me who I am. Yes, there are some days I say I have regrets, but each step has made me change, heal another part, learn a new tool, meet someone new, or move. Each step really has been a blessing, even though it doesn't always seem like it.

Counseling was good, but it was not helping move through the root cause and what my body was holding onto. I also spent time at church youth groups or Young Life because I knew there was something out there bigger than me, but I struggled with church because I was taught a lot of shame and guilt there. I felt like I was always sinning and had to be forgiven. Between that and the patterns I grew up with, I became the people pleaser – saying sorry A LOT; always seeking approval; trying to do the right thing; always trying to be perfect. While living with the criticism I started to give my power away and became silent and just accepted the negativity. I ended up in a dead-end toxic marriage, and had to always be busy to keep the peace in the home. I was worn out from being a single parent (my husband was not around much), working overnights to "contribute" something to the household, and taking care of the children. I started to burn out and was not happy with how my life was going.

My first big step forward was taking the "Awakening Your Light Body" meditation class created by Orin & DaBen, and it was a life-changer. It was a very deep, intense, healing meditation class that helped me start bringing my power back, healing my inner child and heart, learning to find my voice again, and opening up my intuition and guidance from God, spirits, angels, and the Universe. It connected me to my higher self, and things finally started to make sense.

The quote "Praying is talking to God, meditation is listening" deeply resonated with me. I heard guidance, and it was healing blockages, walls, and imbalances held within my body. I realized I had been closing my body off from all the traumas I had experienced. I used to wear a hat all the time, a turtleneck as much as I could, and would stand hunched over with my arms crossed. It had closed off my heart, my voice and my connection to my intuition. These days I rarely close those parts of myself off, and when I do I am immediately aware of it and can shift.

The meditation started to open the channel from the root all the way to the infinite. Just like a tree, the roots are wide, deep and supportive; the trunk is the thin channel, the fine line that creates balance and then blossoms to the infinite possibilities that are ahead of us. We have to keep the channel open, aligned, and strong to keep everything together and flowing.

The work I was doing and steps I was taking did change the path of my life. "My spirit irritated others' Demons," meaning it caused a lot of conflict and frustrations with people in my life. I was no longer in alignment with them and I was not the people-pleaser anymore. I was standing my ground. I was connected to my higher purpose and my soul. I left the marriage because I wanted to walk the walk. I wanted to show my kids how to stand up for themselves, to find courage and not let anyone treat them that way. I also became more open with my children, and encouraged them to communicate, be comfortable in their own skin, and go for what they want. I sometimes had to accept that they could only understand at their level of perception; no matter how hard I tried I could not get them to understand or force them to do anything. I had to let things go. It was their journey and family patterns that they would have to address and work on themselves.

My children would also be my biggest helpers over the years, often guiding me to the next class or mentor that would help us grow and heal. I was so grateful for all these teachers shared, showed me, and opened me up to, especially about being an Empath, Spirits, Angels and Guides, Body Talk, Mediumship, properties of stones, and past lives and the effects it has on our life today. The more I studied, the more similarities I saw in different modalities. I was peeling the crap away and uncovering my authentic self. I could see more clearly why people act the way they do, the things that had happened to them to cause their emotional body to get stuck or blocked. It was so intriguing and fulfilling to finally understand things.

The other tool I depend on and use that made a huge difference in our lives is Trailblazing Communication. When I had my moments of struggle I usually was alone; people were too busy or didn't want to be bothered, or I couldn't afford the help. The best part of both meditation and Trailblazing is that I can do them myself, at any time, without having to depend on anyone else. It takes time and bumps in the road to shift through the stuckness, struggle, block, and misunderstanding, but the more I use these two tools the more clarity, understanding, and a-has show up. Life gets better and more balanced.

Trailblazing Communications uses a pendulum, an internet program, and spirits and guides to help shift through patterns and blockages. Tara Argall designed and created the program. She was a counselor who transitioned to "body talk" to shift people's energy. It is unbelievable what the body stores, the experiences, the thoughts that get trapped there, what beliefs are causing us to be in "dis-ease."

The kids and I went to Tara for years to help us shift through all the trauma the divorce caused, then one day she introduced me to the program so I could do the work myself. This program has so many different facets to it. Through it we can work on the land, pets, ailments in the body, patterns in the family, along with people who are non-verbal – all by asking questions, guidance from guides and their higher self so they have a voice. I resonate most with the program by tuning into families and helping them clear and shift the ancestral and genetic patterns. I work on patterns going back seven generations. I can see the pattern that is passed down and am always fascinated by how the timelines are so closely related. This work is so important, as it helps ensure that future generations don't continue the trauma and instead expand and grow more than they thought possible. I teach them to not shut their gifts and intuition down, and to live in peace and happiness as their authentic selves. I teach them that they don't have to wait as long as I did to find peace, joy, contentment and possibilities. Do I still have moments when I get stuck? I do, but I use the tools to bring myself back into balance.

We all have our own journey, free choice and free will, and we may continue to make painful choices. This is how we learn. We do have to take responsibility and ownership; to work on ourselves and our kids to heal those patterns, that illness in the family, and the blocks we have in our bodies. It starts with peeling away the layers so we can let go of the baggage, ideas, and beliefs and find our true selves. It is still tempting sometimes to blame others for all the hurt, but I have learned to keep walking forward and doing what I can to heal myself.

Is your life out of balance? If so, it may be time to start finding tools. Start taking classes. Start finding what makes you happy again. Start healing those family patterns and healing yourself. Plant the seeds and watch your life grow, bloom and bear the fruit of the work you have done.

Jill Tyge is a mind, body, spirit coach; Awakening Your Light Body meditation teacher; Trailblazing Communication practitioner; author; Young Living distributor; Ayurvedic Body therapist (including Shirodhara and Marma therapy); and owner of Pura Vida Peace, LLC. Jill helps people become their own perfect partner and create balance in their lives. She identifies ancestral/genetic patterns passed down through her clients' families and clears them via energy work. Through meditation, Jill teaches her clients to increase their power base, heal their hearts, find their voices, and manifest the lives they desire by opening the channel in their bodies. She goes deep to address the root cause of things that are holding them back, find what is buried inside, heal what is causing unease, open the heart and become aware of their true purpose in life. While she loves her Trailblazing sessions, Jill also likes to pass on the tools that have helped on her own journey so they can continue the work themselves.

Tyge enjoys the outdoors, boating, hiking, skiing, traveling, cruising, listening to music, and entertaining family and friends. She resides in Belleville, Michigan with her husband.

JillTyge@gmail.com

JillTyge.com

YES, YOU ARE A HEARTIST!

Lisa Eleni

When advertising my artshops I inevitably receive responses from people claiming that they aren't creative. "I am not an artist," they often say. This is hard for me to hear because art and creativity are such a huge part of my identity. As I open up the conversation, I discover the layer of fear or judgment, or the activation of a trigger because someone criticized their expression of creativity long ago. "The purple tree should be green" or "It's not colored within the lines" are wounding words to any budding artist because they can block free expression. Creativity comes in so many different forms and can be expressed in so many ways – it is just a matter of finding what flows naturally for us. Limiting beliefs about what constitutes creativity keeps us stuck in the head, where judgement resides; therefore, I encourage those claiming they are not creative to drop from the head into the heart, for it is there that they will find their unique artistic expression, which I call "heartistry."

I am an intuitive artist, and I create monthly heartshops that encourage participants to live a life of intention in creative ways. Each month focuses on a different theme and art project. The art is not about making something deemed fit to sell on eBay; it is about a personal expression – from you, to you. It is an opportunity to create a visual piece that inspires you to stay aligned with your monthly intentions; it also prompts participants to allot time to relax and to tune into their heart energy. I have never had a guest complete their project and be disappointed with their creation, which is a great confirmation that art is inside all of us. In fact, even the most reluctant participant is inspired by the variety of supplies to create in a safe environment, free of criticism. That is the key to releasing those creative juices and letting your excitement and the wonder guide you toward an amazing outlet for your artwork and your heart.

Creativity became a focal point of my life in my thirties, when I had young children. I have always had artistic tendencies – as a high school teacher I remember spicing up my curriculum by emphasizing the "art" in Language Arts class – but it wasn't until I was raising kids in a small rural town that art became a way of creating a sisterhood.

In an effort to spend time with other adults while also being productive, my friends and I created the Bitch and Stitch Craft Club. Each woman from our small circle chose a different month, chose a craft, put together the directions and supplies, and hosted the group. Everyone brought the snacks! This was back in the 90s, before Pinterest was a household name, so coming up with a DIY that we all could actually enjoy was often challenging, especially when there was no major holiday to decorate for. Still, there was always something amazing that was created each time we got together. While the craft was something we could all incorporate into our décor or holiday decorations, it was also an amazing time for us to bond about our family and work lives. None of our artwork was the same, and none of us were professional artists, yet we all created a unique rendition of what we had chosen for our monthly craft. We shared recipes and cold remedies and scheduled playdates, with and without our children. It became more than a craft club; it was a time to create connections and bonds with each other that spilled into our other life experiences.

We spent time at church functions, at each other's homes, cheering for each other's kids at our small-town sporting events and giving hugs of encouragement to each other when we felt guided. Moms with older kids gave advice to the novice moms who dreaded the inevitable separation on the first day of kindergarten. Sometimes we simply held space for the mom who needed to be heard or the one who just needed to cry or talk about career changes. The sisterhood we created under the guise of a craft club is what has inspired me to begin women's heartshops.

Connection is so important for women of all ages and stages. What I learned is that we are all on a similar journey filled with joy, sorrow, trials, and a little bit of the unknown. There are definite stages that are recognizable in all of our journeys; and whether they be the many transitions a mother goes through, from caring for an infant to helping their young adult move into a college dorm, to the career shifts experienced by a woman who doesn't have children; there is always a heart connection when you are with like-minded women.

You may not be a professional artist, but all of you can call yourselves a heartist. When you generate art from the heart, you are manifesting a creation with a higher vibration and displaying joy as you tune into your imagination and personality and freely express it. It becomes your soul's expression of love. There are so many ways to ignite creativity in your daily life, even without a craft club.

Personalize Your Space

Personalizing your space is a great way to connect with your inner heartist. I'm sure you started in your teen years with posters, random pictures and even vibrant paint color in your bedroom. I remember my daughter painting her room with her friends to reflect her emerging personality more than once! To most teens, a bedroom is a private sanctuary to chat on the phone, do homework, and deal with the turbulent emotions of the adolescent years. Even bringing your own personal touches to a dorm room is an element of heartistry. The space that encompasses your own expression of your likes and interests is the canvas for your creativity.

Now that you are older, making your house a home is an outlet to express your beauty and personality on a bigger scale. Every element, from the furniture to the floors, is an opportunity for you to express yourself. We have all been in the store and spotted a knickknack that just had to come home with us. Finding a space for the special artifacts that touch your heart is tapping into your creativity as you integrate new treasures into your space. Every little statue, candleholder and windchime around my house seems to tell a different story. I can remember having my feet in the sandy beaches of Cancun with my children every time I look at the flipflop magnet on my refrigerator, and I get a little teary-eyed when I see the footprint ducks my children created in kindergarten framed in my bathroom. Remember, art is in the eye of the beholder, and whatever speaks to you is a perfect self-expression of your space.

Adding personal touches that aren't new are also expressions of creativity and of your heart. Incorporating the doily your grandmother made or the lampshade from your dad's lighthouse sculpture into your living area is a wonderful way for you to connect with your inner heartist. It also manifests a space that is not only welcoming but a reflection of you and your loved ones.

Make a Collage

Anyone with a phone has taken spontaneous selfies and photos that evoke emotions just by looking at them. Even the novice photographer can snap an amazing sunset. Taking the time to print those out and make a collage or put several photos in a dedicated space is a great way to express your creativity and fill your home with those moments in time. Those photos are magical because they aren't thought-out and planned laboriously in your head, but rather capture those unprompted, authentic moments in life.

Make Your Space Festive

Decorating for the holidays can bring joy not only to you but your family and friends as well. When you are creating a space that magnifies the beauty of the season or holiday, you are infusing it with your personality and your excitement about the occasion. I have a friend who transformed her whole house and yard into a candy land each Christmas. It is definitely not the traditional green and red, but it evokes a childlike magic that captures the holiday spirit. Every time you find new ways of filling your space, be it with plants, fresh flowers, pictures, throw pillows or even a new paint color, you are sparking your inner heartist.

Spice Up Your Kitchen Routine

The kitchen is an excellent space for you to express your creativity daily, whether you are trying new recipes or putting together the family favorites. If cooking everyday has lost its luster, adding fresh herbs from your garden or making bunny pancakes for your little ones can reignite those creative urges. My kids used to get excited when I arranged their food in animal shapes on the plates. Seeing their smiles and hearing their giggles make the daily grind into a new fun adventure. Trying new decorating techniques for cupcakes or new desserts can be a great way to express yourself too, especially if they are for a special celebration. Any change in your daily food preparation routine can reconnect you to your creativity, and there are so many places to get inspiration – from cooking shows to recipes online to celebrity cookbooks. Start by designating a "new recipe night" each month and put your heartistry to work.

Accentuate Your Look

You are your own empty canvas! A beautiful way to connect to your artistic side is through your own appearance. When you go down the aisle of a grocery store or beauty shop you will notice the multitudes of eye shadows, lip color and hair styling tools. This is a welcoming place to gather up a variety of supplies, connect with your personality, and let it shine! Use new eyeshadows to change the shape and contour of your beautiful eyes. Throw in some sparkles and contrasting lip color and you have created a new masterpiece. It is not a permanent change, but a chance to playfully change the way you interact with the world on any given day. Each morning you can tune into your different moods or challenges to determine how you will style your hair and adorn your canvas with your choice of outfits evoking emotions ranging from whimsy to empowerment. Connecting to your personal style is truly the embodiment of heartistry.

Artistic expression is an all-encompassing term for traditional outlets such dancing, poetry, painting, pottery and sculpture; but it can be alienating as well. Many feel that they are not artistic if they can't perform or create in traditionally artistic modalities. However, being an artist is more than manipulating your body to perform or filling an empty page or canvas. The one thing all of these mediums have in common is the connection to heart energy.

You may not be a professional artist, but when you are in the heart space and elicit change or emotion to enhance your space, food or even makeup; you are a heartist!

Lisa Eleni is an intuitive artist, author, and Mind, Body, Spirit practitioner certified in Angelic Reiki and Theta Healing. Her passion is encouraging adults who desire a more joy-filled life and who want to manifest joy with daily intentions and some artistic expression!

A Massachusetts native, she currently resides in Colorado where she engages in heartistry intention classes to hold creative space for likeminded people to befriend and support each other. She has two adult children who her biggest supporters and inspiration for authentic and intentional, art-filled living. Find more about class blogs, spirit art and tree readings at lisaeleni.com

DESIGN YOUR BEST LIFE BY LIVING FROM YOUR YES

Dr. Lisa Thompson

Imagine living a life where you are able to move forward with inspired action steps that come from your soul, rather than your logical mind or somebody else's desires. What would that look like? What kind of life would you create?

We all have the ability to consciously design our lives, whether we realize it or not. When we learn to pay attention to and trust our inner wisdom, we are in flow with the Universe and our lives are filled with ease and grace. We are able to determine what people and situations are right for us and those that are not. We make empowering decisions and stand firm in our own truth and power.

For much of my life I felt like I was living on autopilot. Though I got intuitive nudges and insight, I would often ignore or override them with my logical mind (usually out of fear), which kept me stuck in careers and toxic relationships. I was definitely not living my best life.

Things began to shift seven years ago after I was introduced to Human Design by a friend. Intrigued, I engaged a Human Design coach who read my chart and helped me to understand how my specific Inner Authority (intuitive wisdom) could be accessed. It was a life-changer! I started working with oracle card decks and pendulums as additional tools to access my inner wisdom, and I took classes to deepen my intuition. The more I used the tools, the more I began to trust that I had all the answers I needed.

Since then I have been able to transform my life into one I absolutely love, simply by following my inner wisdom and living from my yes. I divorced my second husband and am now happily married to the love of my life. I also transitioned professionally, from full-time interior designer to spiritual teacher and Past Life Regression coach, and I use Human Design to help my clients as well. I eventually sold the design business I'd had for twelve years, and recently moved from rainy Washington State to the Big Island of Hawaii. These are just some of the changes I have made.

Now, when I get a "yes" about which direction to take, I don't hesitate like I used to. If I get a no, I honor that and keep the boundary for myself. Life is flowing beautifully since I started living from this empowered place, and one of my missions is to support and empower other women to embrace self-love, trust their intuition, and gracefully move through their fears to take inspired action. Below, I share with you three powerful modalities to help you access your own inner wisdom and design a life you love.

Getting to Your Yes with Human Design

According to Human Design, each of us has a specific blueprint for this particular life, including the way we naturally get an answer to a question. This built-in "GPS" system, or Inner Authority, doesn't lay out the entire path before us but rather provides step-by-step direction that gets us where we need to be. Inner Authority is about how we are responding to life. When we use it the way we are meant to the response does not involve language or even the mind. It's an energetic event that has us connected to the flow of life. Using your Inner Authority requires ongoing practice because the logical mind is conditioned to take over. I explain the different kinds of Inner Authority below. To find out what your Inner Authority is, you can get a free chart at www.humandesignamerica.com/chart.

With **Splenic Authority**, your decisions are made as a very quiet spark of knowing through your intuition. You may not know why you're getting an answer in a particular moment, but you must learn to listen for it and trust it, as your answer will only come one time for each situation. You have the ability to make instantaneous, snap decisions when you have the aha moment.

When you have **Sacral Authority**, your decisions are made in the gut with a verbal uh-huh (yes) or uh-uh (no). To get the answer, it has to come in the form of a question from an outside source. A good strategy to use for big questions is to have a trusted friend ask you yes/no questions about the situation, so you can listen for your answer in your gut. You have the ability to make your decision at the particular moment the question comes. Always trust your gut over your mind and be neutral in your expectations of the answer.

With **Emotional Authority**, your decisions are made after you go through a roller coaster ride of emotions about the situation. This could take a few minutes, hours, days, or longer to process your emotions. Your answer is the clarity you receive in the neutral stillness at the end of the emotional highs and lows. If you make a decision before your emotional processing is complete, you are likely to make a decision that is more challenging for you. Pay attention to how you are feeling in the moment and over time. Be patient with yourself as you go through your emotions.

When you have **Heart Authority** (also known as **Ego Manifested** or **Ego Projected**), it is your job to make something happen if your heart wants it. It is straightforward and direct. What do you deeply value? What is your heart's desire? If your heart is not in it, the answer is no. If this answer is yes, it is a deep, heart-felt wanting that is absent of ego.

With **Self-Authority**, your decisions are made through an innate knowing that you can't explain. It is like a flower unfolding in your chest, and can be a very subtle experience that requires spaciousness and a quiet environment in which you learn to connect. When you ask things like "Will this make me happy?" or "Is this the correct direction for me?" listen to the words you say, as that is where you will find the truth.

When you have **Outer Authority (No Inner Authority)**, your decisions are made through an external process. Ideas must be researched and fully thought through over a period of time, and the sum total of the experience gives you your direction. If you are a Mental Projector type, your environment will provide you with sensory information to give you guidance. If you are a Reflector, you will need a full 29-day lunar cycle to experience all possibilities to make an informed decision. Patience and timing are critical.

Accessing Information Using a Pendulum

A pendulum is a tool used to connect to your higher self and Source by asking questions to help guide, clarify, and raise your awareness. You are acting as an energy conduit from Source to the pendulum. Pendulums indicate answers to yes/no questions by moving backwards and forwards, side to side, diagonally, or in a circular motion. For a pendulum to give you a correct answer, you must clear your mind of all preconceived ideas and expectations to what the answer will be. It is important to stay centered and neutral to let the information flow through you.

To get the baseline of your pendulum before you start asking questions, hold the pendulum in your dominant hand so the weighted part is hanging down free. Use your other hand to cup under the pendulum to help focus the energy. Then, place the elbow of the arm holding the pendulum on a tabletop or against your body to keep your hand steady, relax your mind, and ask your pendulum to show you a yes. Allow it to move naturally, and pay attention to its specific movement. Stop the movement with your free hand to reset. Ask the pendulum to show you a no. Once you identify your no, stop it again to reset and ask it to show you a maybe. Now you have the baseline.

Before asking questions, clear your mind. Call upon your higher self to answer the questions, seeking only truthful answers, which are aligned with the highest and greatest good for all concerned.

You are now ready to ask the pendulum questions. Phrase your questions so you can receive a yes, no, or maybe. You may need to clarify your question if you get a maybe by asking it in a different way or asking it with more detail. Concentrate on your question. Remain detached and neutral, only focused on receiving a correct, unbiased answer. When the pendulum swings, look at the direction it is moving. This is your answer.

Guidance from Oracle Cards

Oracle cards are another tool used to ask questions for guidance on specific issues. One thing to note about card readings is the answers given are not set in stone. They are a reflection of what the likely path will lead to, based on where you are in your life at a particular moment in time. I have learned in working with different card decks that the cards never lie. There is always a reason why you pick a particular card or set of cards. Even if you don't understand the meaning in the moment, if you contemplate it, the information will become clearer to you.

As with pendulums, you will want to program your deck's source of information, so you are letting your higher-self or Source answer the questions, rather than your subconscious mind. It is extremely important to be neutral in your emotions when you are using the cards.

There are a variety of ways you can use your oracle cards. I like doing a daily one-card pull each morning, asking what I need to know for my highest and greatest good for that day. At the end of the day, I reflect back on the meaning of the card to see how the information played out for me. I also like using the cards to ask about what I need to know about a particular situation. If I don't understand the answer, I may pull additional cards, asking for clarity. For more advanced oracle readings, multiple cards can be drawn, such as Past, Present, Future and Month-by-Month readings.

Final Thoughts

Understanding your Inner Authority and using pendulums and oracle cards are all excellent modalities to help you access your inner wisdom and move forward in life. Of the three, your Inner Authority is the one that will not fail you when you learn to trust it and follow its guidance. Using pendulums and oracle cards can give you accurate information when you are able to stay neutral in the response and ask for answers from your higher self. The mind is powerful, so if you are not clear and neutral it will sway the answer.

When you fully embrace your life by living from your soul's yes, you will create magic. You don't need to know every step ahead of time in order to reach your goals; just learn to follow step-by-step guidance from your higher self in each moment. Trust yourself and the Universe, and you can absolutely design your BEST LIFE!

Dr. Lisa Thompson is a bestselling author, speaker, designer and intuitive transformational coach whose practice focuses on empowering women to design lives they love. She helps her clients learn how to live from their "yes" so they can embrace self-love, trust their intuition, and gracefully move through their fears to take inspired action.

Lisa is the author of the bestselling books *Sacred Soul Love: Manifesting True Love and Happiness by Revealing and Healing Blockages and Limitations* and *Sacred Soul Spaces: Designing Your Personal Oasis.* She has created six oracle decks and designs intentional jewelry inspired by her passion for travel and nature. She has been featured in spiritual summits including Celebrate Your Life; Quantum Miracles Mastery; and One Heart One Earth Global Awakening.

Lisa leads destination retreats in her home state of Hawaii, as well as in Bali and Thailand. She teaches online courses and workshops, in addition to coaching individual clients to design their best life. She is available for Human Design chart readings and Past Life Regression therapy. For more information, visit www.DrLisaJThompson.com.

JOURNEY TO JOY

Mavis Frueh

I grew up on a hobby farm in rural North Dakota, which my family moved to when I was just a year old. There was a white 1911 farmhouse, surrounded by trees, pastures for the cattle and pens for the sheep. The farm was the perfect place for my mom, who loved to garden, freeze veggies in the fall, and make jams and jellies. She was also a great baker, and food was a source of comfort in our home. Celebrating? Have a special treat. Bad day? That calls for a big bowl of ice cream. Not sure what to give your neighbor? Make them a warm casserole or roast.

I remember climbing up on the chair in the kitchen to watch Mom mix chocolate chip or gingersnap cookies by hand, pausing every so often to check the stained handwritten recipe card. The red checkered Betty Crocker cookbook would come out when she was going to make pies. I can still smell the apple pies baking in the fall, or the pumpkin pies at Thanksgiving time. She would take the leftover pie crust, place them on a cookie sheet and sprinkle them with sugar and cinnamon, and bake them to a crispy light brown. They melted in your mouth and were almost as good as the pie itself. Whenever Mom said "Keep your fork" after dinner, we knew there would be pie. Our childhood shapes us, and thankfully mine was a good one. It gave me many recipes for joy that I would take with me well into adulthood.

My husband and I met through 4-H and started dating in college. We married the fall of my senior year, lived in an apartment for a while and moved to our first house in 1998. We had a small garden near the river, a beautiful plum tree and two big apple trees. We tried our hand at making currant and plum jelly, homemade applesauce and salsa. It would bring back childhood memories for both of us, and it was something we wanted to pass down to our own kids someday.

Though we shared the duties of running the household, my husband and I each had our own area of expertise. He was mainly in charge of planning out the garden while I took care of the baking. Baking was an escape for me. The stress of the day would melt away as the sugar, eggs, vanilla and flour blended together with the mixing fork like my mom used to use. He helped, though it was mainly by serving as taste-tester and doing the dishes. We continued the tradition of gardening and baking after we had our two boys.

Shortly after my forty-first birthday our peaceful existence was thrown into turmoil when I was diagnosed with breast cancer. I had started getting checkups earlier than normal because aunts on both sides of my family had had the disease, yet it still came as an incredible shock. Suddenly my days were filled with appointments, ultrasounds, biopsies, MRIs and eventually surgery and radiation. Our boys were just eight and eleven; it was a scary time for them also.

To say the diagnosis changed my life is an understatement. During my healing process I learned to be kinder with my words, to ask for help, to slow down and to try to find joy in each day. I also had an overwhelming emotional response and felt like I needed to "do more" with my life. Luckily, the cancer center had a wonderful counselor to help me through the anxiety. One realization was that I needed to get out of the job I was in, so I started searching. I looked for something outside of the box, but I found a similar position a little over a hundred miles away.

When we were looking at places to live, I asked my husband, "What is something you've always wanted to do?" He replied, "I've always wanted to grow asparagus and rhubarb." My response? "Well then, let's do that."

Our house hunting took us to many places, but we fell in love with a five-acre farm in Minnesota, complete with rows of evergreens, an open area where we could have our gardens, and a wooded swamp area. It was right across from the state park, and there was a river less than a mile away that would be perfect for summertime floating. From the kitchen and patio, we could look down a row of evergreens towards the woods. As we stood there, my husband said, "This is it," and I knew he was right.

We've been here for four years now, years we've spent cultivating our rhubarb and asparagus which we sell at the farmer's market. Our garden has grown to include beans, peas, squash, carrots, beets, zucchini, potatoes, corn, tomatoes and peppers. As much as our land has changed, I still feel a sense of peace walking through those evergreens to the garden. Because of their canopy, the temperature under the trees is normally about ten degrees cooler, and the air is usually still and calm, which is refreshing to me after growing up in the North Dakota wind. As I'm writing this, several deer are walking through the backyard. There are squirrels running around and the chickens are enjoying the fresh air. Working with the land is healing for both of us, but it feels like a ritual for my husband.

Rituals meant something different to me when I was growing up. They seemed scary or dark. I pictured a dark basement or something unrelated to God. A friend explained a ritual as 'something you do routinely to create calm or peace' and that made more sense to me. What do I do to bring joy? I immediately thought of baking and chickens – not the two combined, of course, but because both things bring me peace. When we moved to the farm, I knew I wanted chickens. It took a little longer to convince my husband, but we eventually got ten chicks from a friend at work. They lived in the garage until they were big enough to be outside in their coop. The chickens know us, especially me, the "treat lady." I also talk to them and hold them, and when they see me coming they pace back and forth by the fence as if they are saying, "Oh, here she comes! Here comes the treat lady!" I must admit, it makes me feel like a rock star. It reminds me of the days when my boys were small and would get so excited when I came home. Even though it was just a normal day at work, to them it seemed like a long time. They would run over and give me a big hug. It felt good to feel needed.

To us our farm always felt magical, but we never gave much thought to how it might appear to others. Last summer, we found out while on a camping trip. It was hot, humid and there was a ton of mosquitos, so when it was time for a hike our boys stayed back at the cabin.

We were trekking along when the person leading the hike announced: "You're going to love this!" Excited, we walked through the brush into the rows of trees. "Here it is," she exclaimed, "Narnia!"

My husband and I laughed out loud. It was almost exactly like our backyard! (Our boys would have been annoyed at the similarity). In our "Narnia," fairy houses are sprinkled around the property. There are some along the evergreen trunks, by my son's fort, by the chicken coop and even by the gardens. If you can see fairies, this is their playground for sure. I still grin when I walk out to see the chickens and collect eggs. Each day, I tell them they are good ladies and thank them for the eggs. I have taken them on walks with a chicken leash, dressed them in holiday outfits and made tutus for them. They are pets with benefits. Each journey out to see them brings joy.

Baking also continues to be a great joy in my life. I've probably made hundreds of pies in my lifetime – for county fairs, bake sales, holiday pies and now pies for the market. The pie I remember most, though, is one I made for my husband when we were first dating. I had talked up my piemaking skills to impress him, and I chose Betty Crocker's apple pie recipe because it was tried and true. I went about it as I always did, including making my homemade crust, sure that it would win his praise. Imagine my embarrassment when he put the first forkful in his mouth and grinned. In fact, he was trying not to laugh! I took a bite and felt the crunch of the apples, which clearly had not baked long enough. I don't know if it was the "failure" that stuck with me so much, or the grace he showed by finishing the whole slice, but that was my last pie to go wrong.

Baking makes me feel like I'm productive, like I'm giving someone a smile in the form of a pie, cake or cookie. It's a departure from my regular eight-to-five job and is relaxing to me. I make my pie crusts using shortening, flour, water and a little salt. There is a special mixing fork that I use to combine the ingredients all together, and I get a "feeling" when the dough is ready. Some days it needs a little extra flour or a little extra water. Rolling the dough out is also a skill. Being able to roll out the crust to a perfect thickness feels like a small success. Joy. Each time I make a pie, batch of cookies, almond cakes or krispy treats, I infuse that joy into the food. I hadn't given it too much thought before; I just assumed it was a common thing. How often we assume other people's lives and feelings are similar without acknowledging our own special talents!

There are some things about piemaking you just can't skip. For example, I need flour and when I bake, I get it everywhere. At the end of the night, there is flour on my apron, on the floor and probably on the side of my face. It's a key ingredient to the crust. It can't be skipped. Dishes are the other thing that come with baking. There are the bowls for mixing crusts, bowls for the filling ingredients, special fork to mix the crust, rolling pins, measuring cups and spoons and a small basting brush to make the top of the crust extra tasty. Dishes. Ugh. If ever I could hire help, it would be solely for the dishes, but they are necessary.

Life is like baking: the mess is necessary. You can't skip over the middle, the messy parts, or the cleanup. You'll get covered in flour and have a sink full of dishes, but in the end, you'll have a wonderful, delicious pie. When I bake I offer a connection. Most people share the pie with someone (although I do not judge if you choose to keep one to yourself because they are delicious). I love seeing people at the market smile when they buy a pie. They talk about bringing it to a friend to have with ice cream or an afternoon coffee break. Joy in the form of fresh blueberry pie – what could be better? (Maybe a scoop of vanilla!)

Each person's journey to joy is different. When I write my weekly blog, I always end it with "I wish you peace on your *journey of enough*." The reason I do this is because I feel like peace is something we are all in search of. Peace can feel elusive, but most of us can think of a time when we felt peaceful. When we find that feeling of being "enough," a sense of peace washes over us. It isn't something we can do once and be done. You may be enough today and not feel like it tomorrow. It evolves over time and can come and go. You don't have to get chickens or bake pie to find peace unless you really love it. Just find *your* joy. Walk slowly through the woods and take a deep breath. Think about the things that make you smile. When you find your joy, it will spark joy in others, and wouldn't that be a wonderful thing?

Keep your fork, the good stuff is coming.

Mavis Frueh is a wife, mom of two boys, a blogger, baker, and a cancer survivor.

A North Dakota native, Mavis recently moved to central Minnesota to work for a manufacturing company. Her family started Frueh Market, LLC on their five-acre farm, where they grow fruits and vegetables for the local farmer's market. Mavis also makes pies, cakes and cookies as well as jams, jellies and salsa for the market.

Mavis has a Mass Communications degree from NDSU, but spent much of her last twenty-three years in the manufacturing sector. It wasn't until her breast cancer diagnosis at age forty-one that her heart turned back towards writing. What began as a way for her to share her medical updates with her family eventually morphed into a blog. She publishes a new post each Tuesday at www.journeyofenough.com.

Mavis has a black cat named Toothless and six chickens (Henrietta, Daisy, Noodle, Sesame, Butterscotch and Fancy Pants). She wishes you peace on your "journey of enough."

Using Aromatherapy to Add Intention to Your Day

Melissa Jones

D on't you love the smell when you are peeling an orange? Have you ever noticed how your mood instantly lifts the moment you pierce the skin and that little squirt is released into the air? If you're a coffee drinker, nothing perks you up like the rich aroma of a fresh pot brewing in the morning or permeating your local Starbucks. There are many other smells that can evoke a similar sensation – Grandma's sugar cookies, the desert after the rain, the salty ocean breeze or earthy forest floor. Smells activate the limbic system, which is your brain's center of emotion and memory. Similarly, essential oils can inspire a positive emotional state, enhance your physical well-being, and even help to create a deep spiritual awareness. This effect is known as aromatherapy. Aromatherapy is an ancient practice of self-healing. When we actively seek ways to look after ourselves, we become confident and empowered in our lives. *Confident* and *empowered* — sounds like a magickal existence, indeed! From boosting your mood, to getting better sleep and relief from anxiety — aromatherapy and essential oils could be the solution you are looking for. Aromatherapy involves inhaling the volatile oils from plants like mint, rosemary and lavender to reap their benefits. You can do this in a variety of ways: directly inhaling (from the bottle)

or rubbing a couple of drops on the palms of your hands and bringing them to your nose; using a diffuser to release the scent into your environment; or even adding a couple of drops to a bowl of hot water then covering your head and bowl with a towel and inhaling deeply and slowly. Essential oils paired with intention make an absolutely unbeatable combination! In this chapter, I will share you with you how to set an intention, then bring in the vibration, the aroma and frequency of essential oils to cultivate a magickal life.

Essential oils are incredibly powerful medicines that can bring bliss to your every day. We all have those mornings when we wake up on the proverbial wrong side of the bed, are dealing with a cold or seasonal allergies, or are just feeling blue. These are the times most people reach for some pharmaceutical or over-the-counter remedy … I reach into my bag of oils.

Now, to the intention. Each morning, before the world creeps in or I check my phone, I lay in bed, put my hand over my heart and tell myself, "I AM okay. I AM safe. I AM loved. I AM intentional." This allows me to start the day grounded in that space. I then start the coffee and fill my diffusers with about eight drops of this or that oil (or a combination of oils), depending on the season or my mood. I add the water and push the button and soon magickal goodness is wafting into the air! If I am working at my computer the diffuser closest to that space might get a blend for abundance, combined with something to help me stay focused. I also set affirmations; for example, if I am working on quarterly goals for my business, I write out something like, "I AM a magnet for financial abundance and prosperity. I AM constantly attracting opportunities that create more money. I AM open and receptive to all the wealth life offers me." I place this affirmation strategically around my workspace and home, in addition to speaking it out loud. Before going to bed at night I fill the diffusers with lavender, cedarwood or peppermint so I can reap their benefits as I sleep.

Please, please, please keep this in mind: these are **NOT** the oils you might find at Target or the dollar store. I only use and recommend therapeutic-grade oils. We are talking about things that are important such as your brain and limbic system, health and wellness, so this is not the time to go bargain basement shopping. Research the best oils and if possible visit the farms where the plants are grown, harvested, and distilled. Is the essential oil company being a good steward of the earth? It is really important (stepping off soapbox now) that you use your best judgment and purchase the highest-quality oils in the market-place.

Setting an Intention Using Essential Oils

Since 2007, at the beginning of every year, I choose one little word. One little word to ruminate on and sit with to learn more about myself. This year my word is *intentional,* so each morning instead of just plopping some oils in the diffuser and sing-songing my way through the day, I think about my intention for that day. This is similar to the minute or so I spend with myself before getting out of bed. Am I looking to create abundance in my business? Do I have projects due? Meetings I need to be on time for? Is it going to be a "SundayFunday," or is it laundry day? Which oils can help support me in those pursuits? Do I need to use more citrus today because I am feeling lethargic, or an abundance blend because I am going to be making client calls?

Now, I'll walk you through the exercise as I practice it. I am going to assume that you have a favorite oil, and that you can get it in your hands. I will be using bergamot, the benefits of which include easing stress and releasing the need for control so I can flow with life more easily. When you can relax and *trust* the Universe to handle the details of any life situation, you can *release* the fear of the unknown and become clear about your mission.

Sitting in a chair or a comfortable upright seated position on the floor, I place a drop of bergamot with my hand over my heart space (center of the chest) and a drop in my palm. I then mindfully rub my palms together, close my eyes, cup my hands up to my nose and inhale the scent of the oil. I breathe deeply half a dozen or so times and allow myself to relax, consciously softening my shoulders and relaxing my jaw. I take a nice deep inhale to the count of six, hold for the count of two, and slowly exhale completely to the count of eight. Slowly, intentionally and mindfully inhaling, holding and exhaling. Softening the belly. As I continue this breathing pattern my cellular respiration will deepen and my brain will begin to slow down to a relaxed alpha state. When I am in that alpha state, my subconscious mind is more open and receptive to the suggestion, "I release the need to be in control, I can easily go with the flow." For the next minute or two I repeat the mantra or statement until I really feel it and believe it, as opposed to just repeating some random words. Once I really feel it, I resume my normal breathing and release my hands to my sides, lingering a moment or two in this blissful space. I then add a couple of drops of bergamot into whatever oils I am using for the day, reinforcing the suggestion with the aroma. I will write out that same affirmation a couple of times and place the notes where they might catch my eye. Each time I see it, I remind myself to repeat the mantra a couple of times, out loud or silently, with measured relaxed breathing. This is incredibly intentional, confident, and empowering!

Need Some Suggestions for Oils?

Lemon: Uplifting to the body and mind. Improves focus. Cleansing to the mind and spirit. Lemon helps release old patterning and opens the heart, resulting in joy and hopefulness with clear thought.

Peppermint: Promotes clarity and energizes the brain. Increases attunement with the soul so that your intuitive awareness increases. Fears may also be minimized, especially those having to do with *motion*. Use peppermint when there is resistance to learning something new or moving in a new direction. It cools and calms the mind and helps eliminate the fear of the unknown.

Lavender: Helpful for relaxation, easing stress, and getting a great night's sleep. Supports healthy skin. Helps you to adapt to transitions by relaxing the emotional mind and body as well as opening the heart. Brings energy to stagnant situations. Fosters communication of Spirit, bringing clarity and intuitive insight if you are willing to open up in a relaxed manner.

Orange: Supportive, calming, uplifting to the heart center. Energizing. Orange helps to release negatively-charged emotions such as self-judgment, obsessions and fears so the emotional body can be restored and balanced and we can see clearly again.

Joy: Inspires us to live through our passions and promotes the emotions of love, happiness and confidence. It also helps us release grief and sorrow.

Thieves®: This is a blend of oils specifically designed to support the immune system, cleanse the mind or the environment when diffused, and quickly purify and cleanse negative emotions and vibrations. Use when you feel you might need extra protection, or when there is uncertainty or panic in the air.

Grapefruit: Cleansing to the aura and mental body, which helps release confusion and mental chatter. Once these are cleared we can be more receptive to our inner voice and intuitive powers; therefore, grapefruit ultimately helps us restore our own power and claim our spiritual purpose.

(NOTE: some citrus oils can cause sun sensitivity when applied directly to the skin, so be sure to use a carrier oil when applying them directly to your skin. Education is key here.)

Essential oils can enhance our lives in profound ways. In addition to helping your home and work space smell amazing, they work on the subtle bodies to improve our mood and our sleep, have a little extra pep in our step during the day (without added calories or caffeine), and support our immune system. In a dry climate like the desert, diffusing oils during the day also adds some much-needed moisture into the air!

For people who practice meditation and/or mindfulness, essential oils can bring a new awareness to your practice. Intentionally breathing, inhaling essential oils and repeating a mantra such as "I embrace abundance and abundance embraces me" helps move your statement into the limbic system of the brain. You don't need to be an essential oil expert to get started, just pick an oil you resonate with and go for it!

Born and raised in the Sonoran Desert, **Melissa Jones** has a life-long love and appreciation for the benefits of plant medicine. Her grandmother always had a garden, and Melissa grew up with her hands in the dirt, learning about the various plants (Her favorite desert plant is chaparral or *Larrea tridentata*, especially after the summer monsoon storms. The smell is unforgettable.). She studied at the Southwest Institute of Healing Arts and is a registered herbalist, aromatherapist and RYT500, having completed more than six hundred hours of yoga training. When she is not formulating a tea, making essential oil blends, or recording a meditation, you can find her with her camera taking photos of plants and nature, and occasionally people. As a graphic artist, website builder, and social media manager she spends most of her daytime hours in front of the computer. In her free time, she and her sister developed and launched Hippie Soul Wellness, which provides tea blends, aromatherapy blends and supplies, life coaching and meditations. Melissa's favorite spot in Arizona is Oak Creek Canyon.

She can be reached at melissa@msjonesdesign.com or visit hippiesoulwellness.com if you are in need of essential oils, supplies or an amazing tea blend!

THE ESSENCE OF THE ELEMENTAL YOU

Noel Manikham

YOU are a force of nature. Yes…you. From the beginning of time cultures across the world have held the belief that there are four elements – Earth, Air, Fire, and Water – which embrace and embody critical energy forces that sustain all life. Each element is of great importance to itself and the others, thus balance between them is essential, including within the physical body. We tend to forget how everything in the Universe – physical and non-physical, seen and unseen – are all intertwined. We also tend to forget there is a fifth element: LOVE. In this chapter I will tell the story of how the spirit world came to help me regain the balance and love I was missing, and how you too can reach that balance of releasing, discovering, embracing and loving again.

I've always lived with the knowing that there was something bigger than what I was seeing and experiencing as "life." As a child, questioning the church and not aligning with the answers left me searching for another religious alternative. I came to the conclusion that there was no right or wrong religion – the simple belief in a higher power was enough. And it would be through this belief that I would come to know and feel touched by that magnificent strength I call Divine Power. You see, about six years ago, my son, then eight, suddenly came down with what everyone thought was a stomach bug. He would eat and a few minutes later he would throw up. This pattern carried on for weeks, then months, until we found ourselves dealing with a full-blown medical crisis in which he was unable to even keep down fluids. After a week in Children's Hospital and a barrage of normal tests results, we were beyond graced to have a chance meeting with a specialist who was a last-minute fill-in for our then current doctor. Finally, we had someone who gave us a diagnosis. It was the worst case of abdominal migraines he, or anyone, had ever seen. But that was all they could give us. There were no treatment options available because his body rejected every form of pharmaceutical medication available, and there just was no other method of healing they knew of.

"Do the best you can" were their parting words to us.

How do you encourage your child to put anything in his mouth and swallow when *everything* but water causes two hours of gut-wrenching pain and sobbing? One day we were driving in the car and he turned to me and said matter of factly, "Mom, I think it would be easier if I could just die. I don't know that I can keep doing this." My heart shattered. At eight years old my son wanted to die to escape the pain he was in twenty-four hours a day. I felt like I had failed him. I was broken.

I started going for walks on nature trails close by. A half-mile gravel path encircling a pond was my favorite, and the animals there that had grown accustomed to people. I would listen to my favorite Yanni selection as I walked and unconsciously started saying affirmations to the rhythm of the music. I talked to whomever would telepathically hear or listen to me, asking over and over for a sign that my son would one day find the relief he so desperately needed. I begged to be shown the way. Days went by and then it happened. As I was walking and affirming, tears streaming down my face, I heard a voice in my head that was not my own. Startled, I stopped the music and listened intently. The voice spoke again and told me to continue walking because the world from which the voice was from was about to soothe my soul. I did as I was asked and was given visions as I heard commands and stories to them. It was a mind journey unlike any other I'd had. I was instructed to remember the experience and continue taking the journey over and over because each time I'd heal another piece of me.

I was skeptical. I had asked for healing for my son, not myself. I continued nevertheless and found that each time I began to feel better about myself and my general outlook. If it could help me, I thought, then just maybe it would help my little boy find the fortitude to persevere. It only took a few days for him to be able to sit long enough to complete the task, and we eventually increased it to several times a week. Small improvements started to happen and at his request we moved to just once a week. Within just a few months he was able to eat without the intense pain he used to feel, and then again a few months later he had only minimal daily bouts of discomfort. Slowly, he began to find vitality and eventually perfect health and unbridled optimism. He thanked me for never giving up and listening to "that voice."

After seeing the incredible changes in my son, I started to use this same method with several of my clients. Each had their own trying situations and were losing hope so they agreed to give it a try. They felt they had nothing left to lose. Each found their own levels of valued success, including the courage to finally begin making the life changes they needed. The following is a simplified version of the magical mind journey the spirit world gave to me. I will share with you the process of becoming, transitioning, and fully embodying a representation of each element. Tune into that which you have become and take note of as many details as you can. I advise you to get some note-taking materials, maybe put on some soft music, and find a comfortable spot so you can fully relax. After you finish your journey, I suggest writing down the following and researching the meaning of each notation.

- Earth: What kind of tree did you become, and what did the bark/leaves look like?
- Fire: What color are the flames, and how are they dancing?
- Air: What bird or flying creature did you become? Did you notice things like broken/scarred wings?
- Water: What was your water animal? Was it warm or cold, what was seen?
- LOVE: How did you experience this? Were you comfortable in it, how far did you travel, and who did you see?

With each elemental aspect there is an associated emotion you will feel. Remember those emotions and how they affected you, as well as what actions, if any, you took during your travels.

Now, take a few moments to relax. This is the only part where I will not give specific detailed instructions or guidance – just do whatever feels right to you within the following outline. It is now time to begin…

Feel yourself transported atop a lush green grassy cliff. Walk forward and see the vast body of water below you. Smell the salty sea air. Look up and see the vibrant blue sky. Now take a few steps back, close your eyes and widen your stance. Firmly plant your feet and feel roots coming from them anchoring you into the earth below. As they sink further and further, your legs and torso start to take shape and become the trunk and body of the tree. You see bark forming and raise your arms above your head as they become glorious branches filled (or not) with leaves. A breeze comes and your branches wave and bend in the wind. The movement of steadily swaying is soothing and relaxing. You begin to feel a pulse in your feet. It becomes stronger and stronger – a rhythmic beat – as the earth's pulse rises up in you. You are now EARTH.

As you sway your branches you look to the sky and notice a flicker. You're captivated and it draws near, touching your highest branch and setting it aflame. As the flame grows and starts to move its way to your base, there is no fear. Protection and safety are provided inside this cool dancing flame. As the Earth continues to pulse up, you are made aware of your deepest fears, your darkest thoughts, and your most defeating realities rising to the surface. There is no escaping the flame as its sets them on fire. It burns away all that has held you back and that which had made you feel less than what your amazing self truly is. Negativity no longer resides in you and falls away. You are FIRE.

The heavy weight is lifted and your trunk begins to break free from the earth and a gust of wind carries you to the blue sky above. As you're transported you transform into a flying being – a bird, maybe a butterfly, or even a flying insect. What did you choose? Feel the freedom as you begin to move your wings and soar through the highest layers of atmosphere. Feel the tiniest of air particles against your body, allowing them to gently mold around and intertwine with your feathers and/or wings. Feel them entering and filling your lungs as you breathe deep. Exhale and repeat each time with a new and refreshing breath. You are AIR.

You look below as you traverse the sky. There lies a sparkling blue vivid body of water glimmering and beckoning you to come for a swim. You fold your wings back and dive fearlessly downward. As you break the surface you transform once again into an ocean animal. Look at yourself and what you chose to become. Take it in for a few minutes and really examine yourself. What does your skin feel like – rough or scaly or silky smooth? Do you have fins? Feel the water touch each and every crevice of your ocean body. Is it cool? Warm? Does it feel wet or have no feeling at all? Then an ocean current nudges and invites you to go for a ride in it. Allow yourself to be moved up and down, around in circles as you gently tumble. Notice other animals you pass, the vibrancy of colors and where you are left when the current drops you. This is about relaxing, taking note, and letting go...going with the flow. You are WATER.

The current softly deposits you next to another of your kind in the massive, transparent blue wet world. You begin to swim and with play with each other not far from the surface – the ease of being with each other is something you quite haven't felt before. It feels soft, gentle, and secure. You glance upwards and see the sun shining down, creating entrancing beams of light in the water. In a swift powerful motion, you gain speed and breach the surface. As you do, you explode into an infinite number of iridescent particles and begin to expand and float to the celestial ceiling. You can feel yourself as one, yet at the same time feel each and every cell separately. Marveling at the glorious nature of yourself, you realize you have reached a new level of emotional attainment and fulfillment. This can only be the feeling of pure and unadulterated love. You are LOVE.

Revel in the newfound feeling as each and every fiber of your being is slowed down...suspended in time and space in a feeling of joy, gratitude, harmony, balance, passion, and bliss – all the summation of divine love –still in infinite particle form. You cannot contain this kind of emotion and want to share it, but with whom? Thinking of someone, you are instantly transported to them and peering in the window to their home. Will they accept or reject you? Pulse your love towards this person and allow them to do with it what they wish, knowing all the while it's in its purest form from you.

It's time to pull those particles back together. Start to take form over the same grassy cliff you took root on. Allow yourself to become whole again, taking in all those particles and come back to the physical awareness of your body.

By connecting with the four essential elements and understanding their presence in and of us, we become aware of our connection with nature and our relationship with the divine love that is who we truly are ... our fifth element. Love is the basis of all things. Learning to love again on various levels leaves us with a refreshed and inspired outlook on life and how we chose to interact with those around us. I invite you to explore, release, discover, embrace, and love again. Feel it, breathe it, let it encompass you, and know it. You and love are one and infinite. Love yourself and you can change the world.

Never underestimate who you truly are and the power you hold within.

Noel Manikham loves to live in a world of all things spiritual, where the magical becomes everyday life. Growing up she was always that go-to girl for everyone with a problem looking for an answer, unknowingly utilizing her psychic skills at a young age. Over the years she expanded her skills and abilities to also include mediumship, medical intuition, guided energy work, and fully embracing and loving the expansion of her empathic side.

Noel is a Certified Psychic Medium through her studies and extensive testing with Lisa Williams and has studied Reiki and Chios Energy Healing, but continues to focus on being intuitively guided during her healing sessions with clients.

When she's not working, she's continues her training with other esteemed masters of her field. Her passion for helping others and assisting them with guidance back to becoming healthy in mind, body, and spirit brings the balance and clarity that unfolds into immeasurable success that is sacred to them.

www.noelmanikham.com

noelmanikham@gmail.com

SPIRIT ART

Rachel Srinivasan

I am continually amazed by the connection between art and spirituality, though I have been shown proof of this connection, time and again, for years now. I have also learned that just like spiritual readings, there is a difference between the information conveyed through mediumship art and psychic art. Mediumship is communication with passed away loved ones and other spirits. These spirits share information with the medium, who in turn shares it with the person they are reading. This is different from psychic information, which is gathered directly from the client's auric field. Similarly, Kirlian photography and aurographs, which capture the subject's life force or energy, are examples of psychic art, while spirit art is actually a form of channeling and is created by a medium who is being influenced by Spirit.

Spirit art often takes the form of painting, drawing, molding or sculpting. During the process the medium experiences anything from a light trance state to being completely controlled by Spirit, in which the medium may have no recollection of creating the art. Many spirit artists have never studied art and create art with their non-dominant hand. There is even the mysterious and contro-versial phenomena called "precipitated art," in which a painting simply appears on the canvas, without the spirit artist ever touching the brushes or paint sitting before them! Spirit artists of historical note are numerous, but some that stand out are Coral Polge, Frank Leah and the Bangs Sisters.

This world would have been completely alien to me when I was growing up. I was born in Tulsa, Oklahoma and grew up in Nebraska, the heart of the heartland. My family never delved into the spiritual realm. We did go to church, but it was a social function more than anything else. We never discussed communicating with the dead or any other form of divination. Some family members, including some of my most favorite, have even warned me against encountering demons! (To date, I have never encountered a demon while doing this work or at any other time.)

Though I have not had a lifelong relationship with spirit communication, I have had a lifelong relationship with art. At one and a half years old, I began to draw – everywhere. I drew all over phone bills and the telephone book. I drew all over my mom's address book and any paper in my vicinity. I once asked my mom and dad to please draw a picture of a lion or elephant. When they refused I became enraged at their artistic ineptitude. I was about three years old at that time.

I was a sensitive child, trying to keep up with the drama of living in two blended households. In fact, one looking at pictures of me back then would rarely see me smiling. Art was my escape from what was going on in my world. When I created my drawings and paintings I would disappear into them. I poured myself into the creation process, and I never wanted people around me as I drew. Their comments were unacceptable unless they had training in art (which was rarely the case as there were no artists in my family), and their bad vibes were always inexcusable.

My sensitivity was not held in high esteem either. Instead, as with most highly sensitive individuals, my empathic disposition was seen as detrimental behavior by a disobedient child. I was often the scapegoat and I also had no role models.

Not surprisingly, I studied painting in college. I also, after suffering a series of heartbreaks, began looking into healing modalities. I needed to know why different types of individuals show up during our lifetime. Why are they here? What lessons do they bring and what made me so vulnerable to them? Through this exploration I discovered the healing practice of Reiki and started attending classes at a nearby energy healing school. When I started getting psychic downloads during Reiki sessions I knew I had to delve deeper to discover what else there was to learn about this mysterious spiritual world. I began studying mediumship and later was recommended to look into spirit art. In 2019, I traveled to the UK with a group of friends to a mediumship camp at the International Spiritualist Federation (ISF). It was a week full of classes, healing, and sightseeing. I signed up for the spirit art and painting classes, which were being taught by Coral Ryder, and I have never looked back. She was an excellent teacher, catapulting me into the previously unknown world of mediumship art. I grew so much during that week and will always feel indebted to the amazing instructors at the ISF, especially Coral.

The most important thing I have learned about giving readings is to trust Spirit. Trust that the message is appropriate and what the client needs to hear. Trust that the images are correct. Trust, trust, trust. Spirit does not waste time and does not waste imagery. I give spirit art readings frequently on my YouTube channel, for private clients, and about twice a month at a local crystal shop. I also read tarot, provide Reiki services, and read tea leaves. Each spirit art reading is different, and each one is special, even if one individual receives multiple readings.

My spirit art evolves as I evolve. When I began my mediumship journey, I did not want to see anything dark or sad; however, as time goes on, I realize that it's just as important to impart these messages as those that are bright and happy. Many people have encountered sadness or fear in their childhood, and even abuse from their parents. This can come through during spirit art.

I've also learned that mediums shut down their abilities due to fear or overwhelming emotions. As I develop, I've allowed myself to more fully express my own sorrow and fear because, again, these feelings are just as important and valid as love and joy. A fuller expression leads to a more accurate reading, on all counts.

I believe anyone can create spirit art; it's just a matter of tuning in, receiving images and capturing the message. First, I recommend having a daily meditation practice. It's very important to be able to center oneself, calm the mind, connect to Spirit, and feel this connection within the body. It's important to be able to do this somewhat easily. A daily meditation practice assists with each of these skills involved in this process. Second, I recommend that spirit artists have a solid foundation in mediumship. During my spirit art sessions, I am intending to communicate with the spirits surrounding the recipient. These spirits can be loved ones who have passed away or are somehow connected to my client; they can also be living people or even guides. I am not depicting my artistic interpretation. During my readings, I am strictly drawing images presented from Spirit and, because each reading is different, I must be open to receive whatever Spirit conveys.

Intention is tantamount. When working with Spirit, your intention is more important than any other factor. It's the same concept when creating spirit art. In order to create spirit art, one must honestly desire to connect to and communicate with the spirit world. The intention is not to have a great story to tell your friends. The intention is not to impress other psychics. The intention is not even to create a great piece of artwork, or a great drawing or a great composition, although it would be nice. The way the artwork looks will be greatly influenced by the spirit that the artist is working with during the creation of the art. The intention of the spirit artist must be pure.

Another tip that helps mediums and spirit artists alike is knowing when they are connected to the spirit realm in a physical sense. The sensation can range from a light tickle on the nose, tugging on the ear, a subtle brush on the cheek, or something similar. I feel a slight vibration with a subtle heat increase behind my left eye. I discovered this sensation when I was studying spirit art. The sensation has not changed as of the writing of this book. Each spirit connection is unique.

About a year after attending the ISF, I was regularly giving spirit art readings with my friends and I told them how I knew I was connecting with Spirit (the sensation behind my left eye). I had started a YouTube channel and was drawing Spirit frequently. Yet I was still skeptical about my abilities, even though I was helping a lot of people. I wanted Spirit to ramp it up to prove that what I was doing was real – that my spirit art and my ability was real. One night, after a full day of readings, I had a glass of wine with dinner and went to bed. When I woke up I felt something amiss with my left eye. I looked in the mirror and was shocked to discover my left eye was almost completely red, just covered in a blood-red hue. Needless to say I was completely freaked out! I had a popped blood vessel in my eye. I woke up my then-husband, informing him that we needed to go to the hospital or the emergency room. My eye did not hurt and I could see fine. Apparently broken blood vessels in the eye are not a big deal. However, I was sure to let Spirit know that the physical signs being given to me are, in fact, real. I need to not second-guess Spirit because I could end up with a red eye or some other unnecessary overcompensation appearing on my physical body. Since then I have never had another burst blood vessel in my eye. Lesson learned.

When creating spirit art, make sure all of your art supplies are with you before you begin connecting. Are you at an easel? Have your paints ready. Are you outside? Have everything set up. Be ready. The connection will be smoother if you are already prepared. Make your intention known to Spirit. Take some deep breaths and get into a meditative state. Once you are there, what do you see or feel like drawing? Maybe there are lines forming on the white paper or a face is visible on or near a wall. There could be thoughts that are not yours coming in. Listen to the message. The message often arrives in the form of images. Draw as much as there is to draw. When you feel that there is nothing else coming in, the session is over. Have patience with this process.

To recap, here are my top recommendations for someone who wants to practice Spirit Art:

- daily meditation (This is important for many, many spiritual practices.)

- a solid foundation in mediumship

- pure intention

- physical connection

- be prepared

Spirit Art is a blessing. It synthesizes my two great loves: art and mediumship. I love doing psychic and mediumship readings, and when I can help individuals connect to Spirit in new ways and give them comfort, it's worth all the time meditating, practicing, and creating art. Understanding mediumship is a must, so join a mediumship circle near you (or virtually) so you connect with others and commune with Spirit in a loving way. Most importantly, let Spirit know of your pure intention to connect and understand how Spirit speaks and works with you. Partnering with

Spirit has profoundly changed my life, and it can change yours too.

Rachel Srinivasan is a psychic medium, painter, professional spirit artist, and Reiki Master Teacher. Born in Oklahoma, Rachel began drawing at a one and a half years old and has never stopped. Her family later moved to Nebraska, where as a high school student she received the Marie Walsh Sharpe Scholarship. She also participated in an exchange program in Rome, where she was immersed in Italian art and language and introduced to oil painting. Upon returning to the U.S., she attended Arizona State University, where she earned two bachelor's degrees, as well as a painting scholarship from the Phoenix Art Museum. After working in digital marketing for ten years, she left the corporate world to focus on her own business. She became a Reiki Master Teacher in 2017 and attended the International Spiritualist Federation and became a professional spirit artist in 2019. Today, Rachel's artwork is exhibited and sold by collectors in Dubai, Turkey, San Francisco, and Phoenix. She lives in Tempe, Arizona with her daughter and loves to surf and paddleboard.

GrandRisingSpiritual.com

SrinivasanGrandRising@gmail.com

MAGICAL SPACE

Sandy Hanshaw

"**S**andy, come outside to run and play with me!" These are some of the first words I remember hearing, probably around the age of four or five. My friend Pablo loved it when I went outside the old farmhouse that I grew up in. We would play in the sandbox and play hide and seek behind the edges of the trees or in the woods near the house. We always had such an amazing time together and he would teach me little games I had never heard of.

Pablo was one of my childhood spirit guides, there to help me through a challenging time after my parents divorced. His purpose was to teach me it was okay to be a kid and not take life so seriously. Pablo and I had so many amazing times and I laughed so hard at our antics. It wasn't until I was about eight that I realized I was the only one who could actually see Pablo. My family did not understand me; they thought I had an overactive imagination and would eventually outgrow my imaginary friend.

Then came the day when we moved to a new town and Pablo quit coming to see me. Heartbroken, I cried every night, not understanding that his job was done and it was time for another spirit guide to take his place. The pain of his absence stayed with me for decades because we had such a strong bond; in fact I can still vividly remember our time together.

After Pablo moved on I could still feel a presence around me but was not able to see anyone. My outer world also changed significantly. My dad remarried and we moved to another house. All the things I loved – being a free spirit, dancing in the grass, staring off into the clouds, and making up funny stories in my head – all stopped. The new expectation was for me to grow up and become responsible, doing chores, staying out of the way, and trying to fly below the radar.

The challenge for me was trying to "fit" the role when I could still sense others around me that nobody else could. This created anxiety and a level of stress that was unimaginable for a ten-year-old. The nighttime was the worst, as I was bombarded with spirits coming to me. I did not understand what was happening and I would scream out for my brothers to help me. Usually they told me to be quiet and go to sleep, but sometimes they would come to my room to see what was wrong. I remember feeling so comforted in those moments.

By the age of twelve the nighttime visits from the dead had become so overwhelming that I began to shut down. It was also during this time that I began to understand I could feel what others were feeling. There was a girl I went to school with who was so lonesome and wanted nothing more than to have friends. I could feel how desperate she was for someone to like her and have someone she could call her best friend. And she was always on the verge of tears, which made me want to cry as well. I was torn; I wanted to help her feel good but it made me feel so bad inside that I simply couldn't be around her.

These early childhood interactions were overwhelming, but they were also preparing me for the life ahead of me. At the time I had never heard of empaths, intuitives, or mediums; I had no words to describe the nagging feeling in the pit of my stomach and the internal voices in my head. Now I know they have been guiding me through life and keeping me safe. This personal guidance system also tells me of things that are going to happen, like the morning my dad died when I knew, even before getting the phone call, that he was gone. It is a gift of love that at times comes with a dash of bitterness.

Clearly my spiritual journey had its challenges, and resources were not readily available to me in the conservative Midwest. Honestly, I did not even know where to look. My priority during the early years was trying to figure out what the feelings, thoughts, and mini movies in my head were and how to turn them off. As a teenager I discovered alcohol and this became a handy tool for many years. Drinking helped me shut down.

Fast forward two decades, to the middle of my divorce. I vividly remember the day I broke down in tears, feeling like a failure as a wife, mother, and as a human being. I was sick and tired of being sick and tired. As this pity party raged in my head, something incredible happened. There was a flash of light and a hum in my ears. My body felt warm as it was enveloped into an energetic hug from Spirit. This was the day I took charge of my life, started to become my authentic self and sought out my magical space.

There are a multitude of ways to find this magical place; connecting is different for each person and figuring it out requires some work. Ego will likely try to step to the forefront and create a curtain of doubt and self-sabotage. This is normal. Change is scary and ego is here to protect us, or so it thinks. Our job is to learn to identify when it comes forward and to find a way to strike a balance within us.

Do people tell you their life story in the checkout line? Are you the go-to person for everyone's problems but they are never there to help you? Do random people tell you their deepest secrets for no apparent reason? Do you attract narcissistic people? These are all examples of the Universe letting us know we need to cleanse and ground our energy. Below I share a few quick exercises that can be easily incorporated into your daily life so you too can find your "magical space." They will create an immediate shift in your energy, not to mention your day-to-day life and how you view the world.

The best advice I have ever received and want to carry forward is to release all expectation about what something is supposed to look like. Just get out of your own way and be present in the moment. Just feel it.

Each day, when you are taking your shower, follow these easy steps:

1. Stand under the water and visualize your body as being gray in color.
2. As the water washes over your head and down your body, visualize the water moving the gray color incrementally down your body towards the drain of the shower.
3. The gray color is being pushed down while the empty space is now filled with a beautiful white glistening light.
4. Once you are full of white light ask Mother Earth to take the gray energy you released and repurpose it into the universe.
5. Now, as you are visualizing your body filled with white light, notice a stem pop out of your belly button. It is your favorite color, and this stem is going to create a bubble around you.
6. Take a deep breath in through your nose to the count of four. As you release it, also to the count of four, you are blowing up the bubble from the stem at your belly button to create a bubble around yourself.
7. Continue the breath work until you are fully engulfed in the bubble of protection.

8. Share gratitude for the energy being repurposed and set your intentions for the day or say affirmations. Take a moment to enjoy the connection.

Another favorite energy cleaning and grounding technique is as follows:

1. While sitting or standing, place your bare feet in the grass and allow the contact with Mother Earth to transfer her loving energy in exchange for the stagnant energy with the body.
2. Close your eyes and allow all of your other senses to engage. Hear the surrounding noises, breathe in the smells, taste the air, and feel the energy movement within you.
3. Visualize the stagnant gray energy dispensing into the earth and being replaced with all-encompassing white light.
4. Take a deep breath in through your nose, and as you exhale through your mouth visualize tree roots coming from the bottom of your feet.
5. With each exhale the tree root strengthens and gets longer until the tree root engulfs your body to your waist and goes through all of the layers of the earth and snuggly wraps around the earth's core. There is no set number of breaths so just do as many as you need.
6. Once you have visualized your connection with the earth, take a moment to feel the connection, show gratitude and thank Mother Earth for the energy exchange and ability to ground your energy. In this moment feel the energetic hug you are engulfed in and sit with it for a few moments.

Both of these exercises can be done within a few minutes, but take as long as you feel you need to. Another way to help with protection and grounding is the use of crystals. Regardless of what technique you use, it is important to see the signs within yourself you need to cleanse, ground and take some time to take a moment for yourself.

The spiritual journey is lifelong, and everyone has their own abilities and purpose for this lifetime. Wherever you currently are on that journey, creating space for your own wellbeing needs to be one of your highest priorities. If your energetic cup is not running over, then it is necessary to continue to do the work to refill it. You cannot share what you do not have.

This is not always going to be easy. We live in a society that pressures us to always have a full schedule, be it with work, kids, friends, et cetera. This lifestyle does not allow us a moment to figure out who we are or what we are passionate about.

Society also tries to fit everyone in a box, rather than allowing people to be their authentic selves. Can you remember in high school when they asked what do you want to do with your life? The anxiety this caused stuck with me for years because I thought I had to decide the rest of my life at the age of eighteen. Well, I am still trying to figure out what I want to do for the rest of my life; the difference is I now see this as an adventure rather than a failure. So far, the journey has been absolutely amazing. Through hard work I have released the expectations of what others think I should be and am embracing who I really am.

I encourage each of you to set aside ten minutes of your day to cleanse your energy and reground yourself. Allow yourself to release all expectations and simply connect to your inner self. Love yourself for the amazing soul that you are!

Sandra "Sandy" Hanshaw is an Intuitive Life Coach; Intuitive Energy Therapist; and Integrative Healing Arts Practitioner. She is passionate about assisting others to find their purpose and truth through education and self-discovery, while using her unique combination of humor and intuitive, compassionate and practical guidance.

Sandy is a graduate of the Southwest Institute of Healing Arts. She has over twenty certifications, including Usui Reiki Master/ Teacher, Transpersonal Life Coach, Angel Intuitive Guidance, Mindfulness Guided Imagery and Meditation Facilitator, and Certified Belief Clearing Practitioner. She offers her gifts as an intuitive to clear energy and empower clients to find the best version of themselves.

Sandy enjoys traveling to new places to meet new people and satisfy her need for adventure. She lives in Oak Ridge, Tennessee with her husband and fur babies Jackson, Bullet, and Bernice.

sandy@sandyhanshaw.com

www.sandyhanshaw.com

PLAYING IN THE SHADOWS

Sarah Berkett

Running with the night, playing in the shadows, just you and I... These are a few lyrics from Lionel Richie's song "Running with the Night" that was released in 1983 and hit number seven on the top 100 music charts. I loved this song then and love it to this day. I always asked myself, *Just you and I? Or is it just me playing in the shadows?* Not only was I playing in the shadows, I was the one hiding in those shadows while everyone else seemed so together, or so I thought. I could not let them see the real me, for I did not know who the real me was, or did I? I was the black sheep in my family, the weird kid at school, the lost soul in life, the one who always had that sick feeling in the pit of my stomach.

As a small child I was enrolled in a private school where the nuns were very strict, to say the least. I am certain this is when I started hiding in the shadows to escape being called on just in case I gave a wrong answer or forgot to turn in my homework. At recess time I stayed back in the classroom and I was the last to leave after the school day was over. I was so afraid of my uniqueness at this stage of my life.

At home, I could not wait to get away and hide in my room where I felt safe and myself. My mum always told me "children should not be seen or heard." My father told me I was his shadow, because I was always with Him. I never took offense because he said it in a loving way and I loved being that good shadow. Another example of a good shadow is a faithful dog that follows behind you all day.

The dictionary defines a shadow as a dark area or shape produced by a body coming between rays of light and a surface. A shadow is a dark area on a bright surface. It is caused by something blocking a source of light. A shadow's outline, called a silhouette, will have the same shape as the object blocking the light.

We're all meant to be more than we currently are – each and every one of us. Do not hide in your shadows, do not hide in your fears, just do not hide. Run past your shadow, run into the light, run through those barriers. Break past the walls and all the shit in your way. Be who you are meant to be and show the world who you are, now. Drop all the baggage. Throw out all that doesn't add meaning. Let go of who you do not want to be. Stop pretending to be something you are not. Do not hide in the comfort of today's social norms. Be who you are, become who you want to be. It will be hard at first. Society likes to create this sense that everyone is the same, but the cold hard fact is that no one is the same. We are all unique. If we try to be the same, the only person we are fooling is ourself.

You will need courage to break past your shadow. You will need courage to break past society's norms. You will need courage to show the world who you are. Fear is what stands in your way. The only one who can break past fear is you. So what are you doing? Why are you still standing there? You know what you need to do. Start doing, start being, start living.

Carl Jung teaches us that the shadow is an innate part of the human being, but the vast majority of us are willfully blinded regarding its existence. We hide our negative qualities, not only from others but from ourselves. To do this we so often criticize and condemn others to ensure our focus does not fall on our own faults and destructive tendencies. We go through life with a false air of moral superiority and a belief that while others act immorally and destructively, we are wholly virtuous and always in the right. It's interesting, the control our unconscious mind has on us.

It has taken me almost ten years to learn how to leave my shadows behind. I was blessed to have met a real-life angel at International Angel Day in San Francisco in September of 2011. Since then I have met hundreds of Lightworkers all over the world through mentors, social media, various events, spiritual retreats, famous speakers and autholy.rs. This journey has proven to be an amazing one, and I continue to grow each and every day.

If you find yourself still lurking in the shadows, I highly recommend that you try some of the following exercises daily.

Become mindful. People who have more self-love tend to know what they think, feel and want. They are mindful of who they are and act on this knowledge, rather than on what others want for them.

Practice good selfcare. You will love yourself more when you take better care of you and your basic needs. This includes, exercise, good nutrition, proper sleep, and a healthy social life.

Concentrate on what you need first and stay focused on it. This will turn you away from those old behavior problems or patterns that get you into trouble and keep you stuck in the shadows.

So many of us continually put ourselves down. Recognize that Source, God, or your higher power – whatever you like to call it – wants much more for us than that. So, how can you help yourself move out of the shadows? Let go of the idea that you have to be perfect; you already are. Live in the moment, every day. Practice gratitude. Come on now, you can do it.

Get some self-confidence. What exactly is self-confidence? Is it an attitude? A belief? A state of being? Self-confidence can be an attitude about your skills and abilities. It means you accept and trust yourself and have a sense of control over your life. You know your own strengths and weakness well, and have a positive view of yourself. Self-confidence is also understanding your own judgments and abilities, and that you value yourself and feel worthy. Do not worry what others seem to believe about you. Try the following exercises to boost your self-confidence. Talking with others is important, so maintain eye contact while you are speaking. Try not to fidget or look away while the conversation continues, as this can make you appear distracted or nervous. Keep track in your journal for at least sixty days; if you do not have one it's a great time to start one. You will be surprised at how much more confident you will have become.

Just the other day some friends and I were speaking about self-love and how many women really do not like themselves much. One friend was really surprised by this, because it's not something women often talk about. I know because I have coached women and have had many open up to me. They try to like themselves but something causes them to still feel that they are worthless, which is why they stay in those shadows. Actually, many women do not even realize that they feel this way. Yet, some of their current challenges are due to their self-hatred or disapproval of themselves. Self-love is a hot topic, so many women do not feel worthy of their own love. Most times they seek to feel worthy through others and this is how they end back up in the shadows.

The following is an activator of sorts that one of my mentors had me do a few years ago. I still do it to this very day, as it keeps me accountable for myself. Get a photo of yourself from six years old or under and look at it every day. Put it in your purse or have one on your work desk or night table. When you catch yourself being critical of yourself, this is who you are criticizing. Your younger self at that time knew you were lovable exactly the way you were and did not have any insecurities. This little girl still lives inside of you. If you can connect with her eyes in that picture, you drop right from your head and into your heart, out of the shadows. This is one of the fastest tools that moves you from self-criticism into self-compassion and self-love. When you are in this place of self-love you are more likely to have kinder thoughts and be courageous.

You must also be aware of your monkey mind and self-talk. Notice when your inner critic or negativity comes up. Do not criticize the inner critic, as it does not help the self-love part. It just creates more criticism and judgement. Bring in that compassionate part of you and say, "Hey inner critic, I know on some level you are trying to protect me, but it is not working. This is not the way I want to talk to myself, nor do I want to stay in the shadows." We are so hard on ourselves without knowing it because it has become a habit to think and be this way. It is not you, just a part of you. You might also set a reminder on your phone to ask yourself, "What is my self-talk right now?" If it is not empowering, choose not to judge or feed into these thoughts; just change directions by choosing another thought, one that is uplifting and allows you to step out of the shadows.

Sarah Berkett is the founder of Beamers Light, a soul-inspired temple of truth, magical awakenings and holistic teachings. She is a Professional Spiritual Teacher, Animal Intuitive, Angelic Life Coach, Reiki Master, Author and Visionary committed to bringing light and healing into this present realm. For the past thirty-four years, she has traveled extensively and has been trained by some of the top experts in her field. She is also versed in many types of healing modalities. She has served clients all over the world as both a Sacred Soul Animal Intuitive and Angelic Therapy Coach. Sarah invites you to visit her website at beamerslight.com

THE MAGICAL POWER OF WRITING

Shanda Trofe

I believe our ability to write is one of the greatest gifts we can receive during our lifetime. The written word is an incredibly powerful tool, not just for those who consider themselves to be writers, but for anyone with the desire to pick up a pen or connect with a keyboard in an attempt to share, create, persuade, or self-reflect.

Writing gives a voice to those of us who feel passionate about helping others transform their lives or thrive during tumultuous times. It's a portal through which we give them a glimpse into our world, thoughts, and beliefs. It doesn't matter if you share through a blog, on social media, or by penning a transformational book or a memoir – if you feel strongly about inspiring change or perhaps just being heard, publishing your writing for the world to enjoy is a powerful place to begin.

The pandemic of 2020 is a testament to just that. As a publisher and author coach, I was fortunate to have one of the busiest years in my nine-year career as aspiring authors came out of the woodwork. My company, Transcendent Publishing, published over sixty authors in 2020, and most of them had this theme in common: they felt a strong calling to get their book published because, given the state of the world, they "knew" their message was needed now more than ever. What a blessing it was for me to give a voice to those authors and help them share their unique messages with those who could benefit from the information.

Of course, not everyone is ready to share their writing publicly, and that's okay. There are many ways to benefit from the magical power of writing, even when we are writing for ourselves and have no intention to ever share those words with another set of eyes.

One way writing lends us the opportunity to heal our past and process emotions is through the act of journaling. Journaling has proven to be a powerful healing modality for those seeking to resolve past trauma or pain. I've personally used journaling to shift my vibration, discover underlying issues, move past blocks, and process pain I'd long since buried. I've guided my clients to journal to remove ego-based insecurities and fears that arise through the book-writing process.

Additionally, you can use the magical power of writing to attract a new future through manifestation. Writing a letter to the Universe, making a list of all that you desire as if you've already acquired it, or simply writing a "day in the life of my dreams" script are just a few of the ways I've been able to attract some of the greatest blessings into my life such as my spouse, home, vacations, career, dream clients, and much more.

And if you want someplace safe to escape to from time to time, you might create that through a work of fiction. Creating a fictional world and characters can be a fun and rewarding adventure, as these projects tend to take on a life of their own. When I write fiction, I like to begin with a loose outline – I'll take time to flesh out the characters and the world in which I am creating; I'll also make sure I have a plot and underlying theme. Then I step aside and allow the story to unfold naturally. What a rewarding journey to finish a manuscript and reflect back on the wonder you've created!

There really are no limits to what you can do with the magical power of words. I say magical because, yes, words really do hold magic! Just think about it: we all have the same number of letters in the English language to work with, yet how we arrange them into words, and the order in which we share those words, gives our writing a different meaning, feeling, energy and vibration. If you gathered one hundred people and asked them each to write on the same topic, each passage would be unique because each piece of writing would be personal to its author. It holds the writer's essence because how we express ourselves in any form is exclusive to each individual. Nobody else has lived our experiences, felt our emotions, or sees the world through the exact same lens that we do.

There is no limit to the magic we can create when we sit down with the intention to share what's inside our heart, and often we don't know what that is until we connect pen to paper. Have you ever gone back after a writing session to review what you wrote, only to find that the words are nearly unrecognizable? Perhaps you were visited by your muse, as many like to call her. I believe my muse takes the form of a guide or my Higher Self, depending on whom I call upon. But more on that later.

In my work, I tend to attract authors who write primarily on spiritual topics, and many of those authors claim to channel their writing. Some channel ascended masters or a team of guides, while others aren't quite sure where the download comes from; they just feel they are the vessel through which the message is meant to come, and this aligns with my beliefs as well.

I also firmly believe that if an idea for any type of writing project is placed inside our hearts, be it a blog post or a book, we are being called from a higher power to be the conduit for that message. It is our responsibility to then answer that calling and surrender to the writing process. One thing I know to be true is that the idea will niggle at our brain and stir inside our heart until we decide to give a voice to it. And when we do, the entire Universe will conspire to support us on our mission. You may find that the words flow through you effortlessly, as if someone else is guiding the pen (or your fingers if you prefer to type). You might also discover, if you're paying attention, that the people who can support you and help make your dreams a reality show up in your life in perfect Divine timing. Information and resources you need become readily available to you, and the time you didn't think you had opens up once you commit to the project and make it a priority.

No matter what type of project I'm working on, I find I have the most success allowing the words to come through when I create a magical writing ritual. I'll share the process I use myself and that many of my clients and students have adapted as well. You are welcome to take what feels good for you and create your own unique ritual. The key is to create the time and space, set the intention, and get out of your own way so your magical muse may whisper to your soul.

Creating a Magical Writing Ritual

First, I like to schedule time on my calendar when I'll be un-interrupted and free of distractions. If you have a full household, this may be the wee hours of the morning when the house is quiet, and others are still asleep. Or perhaps you're a night owl, so you might do this at the end of your day. I find that my best work comes through at four or five a.m. before my day gets ahold of me, and I expel my energy. Find what works for you, and put your writing session on your calendar.

I like to create a sacred writing space ahead of time by finding an area that's outside of my regular work environment (this is especially important if you work from home). Your sacred space should be inspiring and bring you peace. Gather any tools that will aid in your session, such as crystals, candles, incense, essential oils, a journal, pen or pencil, computer, et cetera.

When it's time for your session, turn off your phone or put it on airplane mode, and if you're using a computer, turn off all notifications so you won't be tempted or pulled from your session when the magic begins to unfold.

I light a Nag Champa incense to calm me. I find that when I'm calm, I'm less likely to give way to the ego-based, fear-based thoughts that tend to arise sometimes when we set out to create something new.

Close your eyes, take a few deep breaths, and visualize your writing session flowing effortlessly in your mind's eye. See your full page(s) of writing before you as you finish, and feel the joy and gratitude in your heart for a successful session full of insights and clarity.

I usually select a white candle to connect with the energy of Archangel Gabriel, who is the angel of clear communication, then anoint it with an intuitively selected essential oil – typically frankincense, peppermint or lemon. As I light the candle, I set an intention for the session and call upon Gabriel to assist me. You may elect to call upon God, your Higher Self, a deceased loved one, your spirit guides, angels, goddesses – wherever your faith may lie. If you're unsure, simply call upon your magical muse, whoever she may be, and invite her to assist in your writing project.

At this point, I close my eyes, hold my clear quartz crystal in my left (receiving) hand and invoke assistance:

Archangel Gabriel/[insert deity], I call upon you at this time.

May the words that I'm meant to share with those who can most benefit from my message come to me and through me with grace and ease. My intention for this session is to receive guidance on [insert topic], and I allow you to open my heart and guide my hands so my most heartfelt writing emerges. And so it is.

Next, let go of expectations and surrender to the process. Pick up your journal or connect to your keyboard and begin writing. Write freely without stopping to second-guess yourself or self-edit as you write. Why? When you switch back and forth from writer to editor, you are switching from the creative side of your brain to the analytical side, and that blocks the flow of creativity from coming through. There is a time and place for self-editing, but it's not during your magical writing ritual. If you want your best writing to emerge, you must silence the ego and forbid it from attending your session. Self-doubt is the killer of creativity. Try not to get hung up on what your reader may think because it's hard to write freely with someone (real or imagined) looking over your shoulder. There will be plenty of time to revise and polish it before you share it with the world. However, this sacred piece of writing is for you and you alone.

Your turn. Go out and create a magical writing ritual that aligns with you. Allow your intuition to guide you to the tools you'll use. Have fun with it, and be open to what might emerge. Even if it takes you someplace other than where you originally intended, trust the process, for that's the magical power of writing at work!

Remember, when you have an idea for a project, however large or small, know that you've been called upon for greater work, and a Higher Power will assist you with that work once you commit and get out of your own way. It's up to you to answer that calling and surrender to the writing process. For when you do, magic will unfold, and that mysterious muse of yours just may show up to guide you ... if you'll allow her.

Shanda Trofe is a bestselling author, consultant, and publisher. She studied Creative Writing and English at Eckerd College before she went on to become certified in multiple spiritual modalities. She believes in combining her spiritual training with her experience in writing and publishing to best guide her clients and capture their vision, both intuitively and professionally.

Shanda believes that a life rich with experience makes for a great message, and her passion lies in helping aspiring authors find their voice and connect to their authentic, heartfelt story.

As the Founder of Transcendent Publishing, Shanda has been helping authors reach their writing and publishing goals since 2012. She specializes in book-writing and marketing strategies for authors, coaches, healers and entrepreneurs. Additionally, she is the best-selling author of several books including *Authorpreneur* and *Write from the Heart.* Her next book, *Self-Publishing Success,* is scheduled for publication in late 2021.

Shanda resides in Saint Petersburg, Florida with her husband, their two fur babies, and flock of backyard chickens.

www.shandatrofe.com

www.transcendentpublishing.com

MONEY MINDSET RITUALS

Suzie McLaughlin

How do you feel about money? For many of us, just thinking about money can bring up strong emotions that cloud our judgement and lead us to either overspend or be overly frugal with ourselves. For example, "I can't afford that, even though I really want it. I'll just put it on my credit card," or, "I have the money to buy this, but what if an unexpected expense comes up? I'll be in hot water then!" Becoming aware of and working with the emotions and body sensations around money can help anyone to reach their income goals faster, with less stress and more ease. When we learn to be "the observer" of our money habits and listen to the clues our bodies are giving us, we feel empowered and confident. The money exchanges we experience every day become a conscious action of choice.

Do you have some money habits, or chronic money thoughts, that you would like to change? Do you find yourself in a rut when it comes to personal finance? Is there a spending habit or a money belief you would like to change? If so, this ritual, or "money habit reset," is a place to start.

I am a teacher and coach to many, and I love my work. My favorite thing to do is help people see the world, including money, in a way they may not have considered before. A common issue I see in my work is the limiting of beliefs and emotion-driven habits that become second nature over time. I've learned, through hours of research and trial and error on my part, that our money habits reflect a belief that cause us to sabotage our ability to reach our financial goals. I have also found that many of us create these habits to avoid sensations we feel in the body. One example is a sensation of a rope tightening in the lower back when there is a big financial decision to make. I will teach you to identify these sensations and be curious about them.

My gift is in guiding my clients to find the beliefs hidden in their actions or thoughts and look at them in a new and objective way. Once we have found them, we have an opportunity to choose. Choosing a new money path is a step-by-step process. One step at a time, we create new habits that empower us to work with money as a tool, not a way to soothe or avoid tough or scary emotions.

Here's a story of how I used this process in my own life. As a young adult, I had lots of time and not much money. This was fine, because I was able to create a life that was just right for me, and it gave me the choices that made me happy, most of the time. Yet occasionally, I would find myself in a spot where I wanted (for example, shoes) or needed something and didn't have the money for it.

When I became a college graduate, I received a credit card with a low limit, let's say five hundred dollars. I would use this credit card whenever I found myself a bit short. As time passed, the amount due kept going up. I was paying the minimum but couldn't afford much more than that. Before I knew it, I'd hit my limit.

Now going to the mailbox was like receiving a death sentence. I knew there would be a bill in that box that I did not know how I would pay. I got sick to my stomach (a feeling of helplessness or no power) and was getting headaches a lot (a feeling of lack).

These feelings, felt as sensations in the body, were making me question my ability to work with money.

Later, in this same mailbox, a gift came that was an answer to a prayer. My grandmother had sent me a check for five hundred dollars! I fell to my knees, shaking. Here is an example of a whole-body shift, starting from the top of my head and moving through my body. I began to cry (an emotional release). I knew this money would get me out of the debt I was in, but more importantly, free me from the feeling of being unsafe and not enough.

I paid attention to the feelings (both the sensations and their locations). That insight is what made me use the gift of money for the charge card bill and not for the new clothes I wanted. It was more important to feel safe and back on solid financial ground, where I was able to become empowered. Often these major shifts use up a lot of our energy; I still remember the feelings of relief and exhaustion in my body after my emotional release. Once I recovered from the experience, I knew what I had to do to create a feeling of safety for myself; pay off the card and create a state of being grounded and secure. Even back then, I knew that if I didn't make a different choice, I would have to live with those body sensations that came from a feeling of disempowerment (stomachache) and the feeling of lack or not being enough in the world I had created for myself (headache).

Below are four fun rituals to try. Each will assist you in thinking about money differently than you have in the past. These rituals will also bring forward any feedback loops from your subconscious that may need a reset to align with the life that you envision for yourself.

It takes time to rewire our thoughts and beliefs, so I encourage you to read through these rituals and pick just one to start with. When that one becomes second nature, then go back and pick another. These are all meant to be a lighthearted way to shift our perceptions of "what is" when it comes to money.

Ritual 1

Surround your finances with gratefulness.

Step 1: Every day look at your bank balance.

Step 2: As you are looking at your account think about what you are grateful for. It doesn't necessarily have to do with money in your account, but with gratitude for all the blessings in your life and how the money that flows through this account supports the things you are grateful for. It is important that both steps are done together.

Step 3: Notice what you felt in your body, and your emotions, as you read this ritual. Did you want to skip this ritual? Did you resist opening and looking at your bank account? These sensations and emotions give clues as to how we are interacting with and thinking about money. Our emotions do influence our ability to attract what we want. That attraction starts with gratitude. It will raise our vibration, and we want our account to share in that high vibration.

Ritual 2

This one is a mantra that keeps those good vibes coming around money in general.

Each time you pay for something or you receive payment, say, or think this phrase:

"There is more where this came from!"

This phrase puts your mind in a place of abundance and brings your mind and body up to that abundant vibration. It may seem silly, but it has been scientifically proven that our thoughts create our environment and how we perceive it. Our perception of our world and what is in it, is key to shifting our relationship with money.

I must admit, this is one of my favorite rituals. It is the first one I tried to shift my beliefs and it really worked for me. Most importantly, it is easy and fun!

Ritual 3

Be aware of the words you use when dealing with money.

Do you ever hear yourself saying, "I can't afford that"? If so, try this ritual for one week.

Step 1: Start to really hear and catch yourself saying or thinking "I can't afford that." This step is empowering because you have taken an unconscious habit and made it conscious.

Step 2: Once you are catching yourself saying "I can't afford that," switch the phrase to "I choose not to buy that right now."

Step 3: Take the time to notice how saying "I choose" instead of "I can't" feels different in your body. Just noticing which feels better and more empowering will help you to continue to do this ritual until using the phrase "I choose not to buy that right now" becomes second nature.

This simple shift can bring more flow of money into your life and you will be able to use that currency in an empowered way.

Ritual 4

Take care of your money. Do you have money lying around? To find out, try creating a treasure hunt!

Step 1: Look for coins in your purse (s), in the cushions of your couch, in your car floor boards or cushions or cup holders. How about the pockets of your clothes and coats?

Step 2: Do you have checks you have not cashed? Put them in your account. Do you have a money jar? Take it to a coin machine and cash it in.

Step 3: Do you have gift cards or gift certificates you have not used? Use them! If you don't want them, gift them to someone else so the money can keep flowing.

Step 4: Just for fun, add up all the money that you found. It can be surprising how much money we have allowed to just lay around. Perhaps create a separate savings account for your "found" money. This will reinforce the idea that money is always there, waiting for us to find it.

We need to take care of our money, because money is an idea and we want to show ourselves that this idea (money) has importance and needs to be cared for.

This is a great ritual to do with family members, especially kids. I have done it myself, and our family used it for vacations and other activities we wanted to do. It is always fun to find money and share in the abundance that is all around us.

Remember, one ritual at a time. Pick your favorite, the one that calls to you. When you have used the ritual every day for at least six weeks, you will be able to feel a shift. You may feel or notice it sooner, but I still recommend that you stick with it for the full six weeks to really give it staying power. Ritual Number 4 is more of a once-in-a-while activity, so perhaps do that one to get the flow going at the beginning of your Money Mindset Journey. As with all rituals, the real power of this work lies within you and your belief in the ability to change those unconscious habits. I believe in you and your ability to create a powerful Money Mindset. You can do this!

Suzie McLaughlin wants to live in a world filled with smiles, big dreams, and wild adventures. She also knows that while smiles are free, fulfilling dreams and adventures require a healthy relationship with money. She built this healthy relationship through an exploration of her inner world, and as an entrepreneur she learned to find money or attract money in both abundant and seemingly scarce times. As a coach and teacher, she helps others take those inner world expeditions for themselves.

The practice she has created involves many different modalities, all with the goal of helping clients to understand what the sensations in their bodies are trying to communicate to them. A welcome side effect of understanding these sensations is a deeper understanding of beliefs that may no longer serve a purpose. Our bodies are so much more than what they appear and have so much information to share with us. Suzie is always excited to share these exercises and tools with those who are curious and want to know more.

In her downtime, Suzie enjoys volunteering as a reading tutor, hiking, drawing and finding out-of-the way places in nature to explore with her family.

www.suziemclaughlin.com

WHEN THE BOUGH BREAKS

Tracey Bradshaw

All I could think when as I was going through this was *My bough has broken.* Like in the child's lullaby, I could visualize my life's cradle crashing in the storm and breaking into bits. The experience I'm referring to a breakdown that encompassed not only my central nervous system and the organs, by my spirit as well. It was the full enchilada.

My story started in the kitchen, where I was doing the simple task of preparing lunch. Just an ordinary day, with the usual chaos – family, friends and to-do lists. Suddenly, as I looked around my home, my ears started ringing, my eyes felt like a curtain was closing in on my vision, and I crumbled to the floor as if my legs had decided to go shopping without the rest of the body. I grabbed my stomach, feeling my heart race, my body tingling everywhere, my mind saying, What the hell? I heard my daughter, who was on the other side of the counter, asking me if I was okay. I thought, *I have no idea*, but when I tried to speak I found I couldn't articulate a word! All I could do was sit there, wrap my arms around my body and attempt to just breathe.

I heard my spirit say, "Calm down, it's going to be okay. Let me take this one over."

Easier said than done. My mind filled with anxiety and my eyes turned into puddles. This was my worst nightmare – having no idea what was going on or how to control it.

You see, I had been in control my entire life, or at least I thought I was. Actually, like most control freaks, I was not in control at all; I was just making decisions because no one else was, which gave me the illusion that if I was in order everything would fall into place.

Well, my brain was full of being in order (chaos), and life had begun to throw wrenches my way, more than apparently my body and subconscious could manage: work, deaths, divorce, moves and all-time high stress. It all came to a head that day in the kitchen. While I looked the same on the outside, I was just a shell. I could not do a single thing.

Then my motherly instincts kicked in. *Keep it together, Trace! You have a child and she is looking at you to be her rock.* Well, her rock had exploded!

Now, let me backtrack for a moment and tell you a little bit about myself.

I have considered myself a healer and a visionary, and I have always heard angelic voices guiding my life. In other words, my norm has never been what others call "normal." I have guided others to healing, I have delivered babies, I have been there when individuals transition. I have seen and experienced things that others will never experience.

This breakdown was very different. It took me into worlds I had never been in before. I truly could not stop it or "heal" it while in the depths of different perceptions. I share this trial and experience to show you that you are never alone. You will find great gifts in your worst dark times; you will find strength that you cannot imagine and you will cherish the silver or gold linings in every step you take.

Over the next few days and weeks I learned invaluable insights that I will respect and cherish for the rest of my life. The beauty of the breakdown was that I was forced to accept the change that my body and heart could no longer manage.

We truly have no idea how powerful we are, or how reliant others are on us, until we are weak, nonfunctioning and cannot string together thoughts, let alone sentences. Friends and relatives attempted to rescue me. Every attempt was appreciated ... eventually, though not so much while I was in the thick of things, trying to find my cradle.

I had friends tell me, "You can't do this!"; "You can't fall apart because if you do our lives will!"; "Stop! Get a grip!"

Some even gave up their daily lives, showed up with groceries, wearing their jammies, and slept in my bed right alongside me.

Other spoke words of wisdom over the phone that will remain with me forever.

I realized I had natural expectations of all the individuals in my life, and realized that was not for me to own or have.

I also had friends leave; I found out my tribe was *not* my tribe. I found that for most individuals if it's not convenient for them they don't or can't show up.

I found that putting a reliance on others was not their strong point.

I continued to talk to myself and would always reach out and talk to friends, both near and far. My fear would get the best of me. I had images of horrific actions that I thought I took. I had plenty of sleepless nights until my precious brain was able to compartmentalize the overload.

I slept as much as I could and when I couldn't I would light a candle, grab a journal and write.

I selected a favorite place to sit when I was awake that I felt safe in.

I allowed help and accepted that menial tasks were not an option. I embraced individuals that were honored to help.

At first showering or bathing was not in the picture, but, oh, how wonderful it was when they were! I used Himalayan salts, Epsom salts, a few drops of lemon oil on my spine, and a soft cloth to wrap in as I soaked in the aroma and healing waters. Most importantly, I adopted my own personal mantra that I use to this day: "Be true to yourself and yourself will be true to you."

The tools became part of a new routine and helped me heal as I processed this breakdown and evolved into the person I am today: one who is more patient with myself and accepting of the natural flows of life.

I allowed my personal healing process to work in different ways and gleaned new healing modalities to share with others.

Here are a few:

- I began to honor my weaknesses as my new strengths.

- I established and enabled boundaries that were not identified before.

- I journaled every message, every thought and started to do ceremonies around different situations.

- I can identify now when one's bough is about to break.

- I can identify quickly and intuitively when one's bough has broken and their next steps, as I have lived through this.

- I gained confidence in my intuitive workings and set standard practices that I know penetrates and has greater impact with my client.

- I leverage many modalities, however the greater gifts in my practice all come from my personal journey.

- Timeline Therapy, EFT (Tapping) Aromatherapy and gifted affirmations are the main resources, though I will introduce others I feel are needed.

This is the same process I use not only for myself, but with my clients.

Timeline Therapy – I ask questions around situations and dates. I focus on keywords I hear from the client, document them, and summarize it back to them. This is where the gift comes – in the realization of subconscious or conscious events. The beauty and the fun comes when we create affirmations and scripts for tapping.

Aromatherapy – I muscle test and work with cranial nerves to identify the best calming actioned oils to meet a client's individual needs. I also suggest bath recipes that everyone enjoys immensely when followed.

Tapping with Tracey – Here we return to the keywords the client and I identified in our timeline therapy. We assess the "weighting" of impact on those words, then together we "create" scripts focused on what the client is comfortable with. Then we begin our tapping routine and script.

Affirmations – These are so fun! I teach the client how to write them, then we practice saying them together. We then further this exercise by doing mirror work.

Some things to remember as you work through this process:

- The brain is a magnificent tool, powerful and never to be underestimated. It protects us in any way it feels it should, including modifying, shifting and altering thoughts, chemicals and actions.

- Embrace and give yourself permission to allow. While some situations and thoughts can be overwhelming and fearful our brain is here to support and honor us.

- Please never be embarrassed of being vulnerable; never apologize for your body's need.

- Embrace your bough! Build it up! Reinforce it with your own personal journey and realize your work is to strengthen your bough so when harsh weather hits it will sway but never break again.

- Use your strength, your warrior wisdom, to maneuver through those storms. Some will be light and some will be strong and go on for a long time. Keep your courage, as your spirit will find the strength to take you through that clearing.

- Meditate and give yourself time to visualize your bough and how it's becoming stronger with confidence, tools, and experience that no one else has. This is personal time for you and only you.

- Use essential oils. I have my favorites, but I use many depending on my environment or particular situation.

Here's my process that you can utilize any time you need to strengthen your own bough:

I use white angelica and do a little calming ceremony with my oils and affirmations.

I place four drops of my oil in my hands and inhale slowly, then I rub my ears with the oils.

I look in my mirror and state, "My bough is strong and filled with wisdom. My cradle is safe and will slowly sway in the breeze of life. I am safe and loving."

With everything going on in our world, this process and others like it are more needed than ever. If your bough breaks, you may feel that you will never come out on the other side. You may feel that this is so overwhelming you don't know where to start. You can't think; you can only cry. So many feelings, emotions and fear ripped through me when this happened. I am here to tell you, you will survive and be a better person when you step back out into the sunshine, the healing waters and the laughter of your heart. You, my dear, are never alone!

Tracey Bradshaw is a Shaman Priestess; Heal your Life® teacher; speaker; intuitive educator; and GRM Specialist who has assisted hundreds on their healing journey. For over twenty-five years Tracey has been doing energy work on multiple levels and has studied and worked with numerous teachers in several different healing modalities, including some spiritual luminaries. Through her combined unique skillset and expertise, she has the unique ability to assist individual clients in their own selective journey. During each session, she is able to assist and hold space for each person, which allows the healing process to begin in a very safe environment.

Tracey is a highly sought-after teacher whose work encompasses every aspect of life. Those she works with have said they never before realized how their spiritual concerns were impacting all phases of their Mind/Body/Soul. She has even consulted on financial issues they were having and tied it back to the "missing parts" of their life. She does this with fun, loving settings in person, groups or over the internet.

tracey@traceybradshaw.com

Thank you for reading our stories, hearing our words, embracing our rituals. Thank you for awakening the wild woman and fueling her passion and desire to express, create, and live a mystical life rich with community and sisterhood.

Together we rise.

If you wish to continue the journey, we would be honored to have you join our sacred online space:

www.facebook.com/groups/wildwomengatheringspace

CPSIA information can be obtained
at www.ICGtesting.com
Printed in the USA
FSHW020027150621
82224FS